轻松学成语

Easy Way to Learn Chinese
Idioms

雍贺 编
Compiled by Yong He

新世界出版社
NEW WORLD PRESS

First Edition 1997
Second Printing 1998
Idea Created by Jiang Hanzhong
Edited by Song He
Illustrations by Liu Tingting and Hao Shuhui
Book design by Zhu Anqing

ISBN 7-80005-341-5

Published by
NEW WORLD PRESS
24 Baiwanzhuang Road, Beijing, 100037, China

Distributed by
CHINA INTERNATIONAL BOOK TRADING CORPORATION
35 Chegongzhuang Xilu, Beijing, 100044, China
P.O. Box 399, Beijing, China

Printed in the People's Republic of China

前　言

　　成语，是中国古代灿烂文明的产物，在现代汉语中仍起着积极的作用，已经成了汉语语汇中不可缺少的重要组成部分。成语简明扼要，具有很强的表现力。

　　近年来，中国与外界的交往日益频繁，越来越多的外国人来到中国生活、工作。一方面，外国人迫切希望了解中国的历史、文化以及语言文字；另一方面，中国人在与外国朋友交谈中，经常遇到这样的问题：有些汉语中的习惯表达法，尤其是成语，很难准确、恰当地译成英语，于是就产生了交流的障碍。

　　本书正是为解决上述问题而编写的。编者精选了现代汉语中常用的八十条成语，中英文相对照，以故事的形式，详尽地说明了它们的出处和典故，并给出了简明的释义。且每个故事配有一幅生动形象的插图，以帮助读者理解和记忆。

　　对于那些正在学习汉语，或是对中国文化感兴趣的外国人来说，本书就象一幅长卷，向他们展示着中国悠久的历史和灿烂的文明，令他们在轻松的欣赏之余，领略中国文化的魅力，同时丰富其汉语语汇，提高其中文的语言和文字表达能力。

　　本书的译者 Scott Hillis 先生是精通汉语的美籍专家，其译文准确、流畅，生动、优美。因而，对于中国读者来说，本书可以作为英语学习的辅助读物。通过阅读译文，读者不仅可以掌握成语的英译法，更可以从中领略到纯正、地道的英文表达法，从而提高英语口语和书面表达能力，以便于更加自如地与外国朋友进行交流。

FOREWORD

Chinese idioms, which epitomize Chinese history and culture, are a treasure of Chinese language.

In recent years, with the cultural and economic exchanges between China and the outside world becoming increasingly frequent, more and more foreigners have come to China for travelling or working. On the one hand, foreigners thirst for gaining knowledge about Chinese history and culture and learning Chinese language; on the other hand, some Chinese people find it difficult to translate the Chinese idioms properly into English when they talk with foreign friends.

This book has been compiled to solve the aforementioned problem. It consists of eighty idioms with one story (both in Chinese and English) following each. They are the most popular ones in modern Chinese usage. To enhance comprehension by foreign readers, each idiom in this book appears in two forms: Chinese characters and *pinyin*. With a vivid illustration matching each story, readers will get a strong impression and a distinct idea of each and every idiom.

In addition to displaying a panorama of ancient China and offering much knowledge concerning Chinese history, this book provides foreign readers with a chance to become acquainted with the essence of the Chinese language. By reading this book and trying to apply the idioms in writing or everyday conversation, foreign readers will find their Chinese friends amazed and impressed, and thus will become more confident in the study of the Chinese language.

Furthermore, this book has been translated by Mr. Scott Hillis, an American expert who is proficient in Chinese language, and thus it presents fluent and elegant English to readers. Therefore, it can help Chinese readers to improve their spoken and written English, enabling them to communicate with foreign friends more freely.

目　录
CONTENTS

按 图 索 骥

àn tú suǒ jì

（按，on the basis of；图，picture；索，look for；骥，steed）

LOOK FOR A STEED BASED ON ITS PICTURE

古时候，秦国有位著名的识别马匹的专家叫伯乐。几十年中，他识别过成千上万匹马。伯乐到老的时候，根据自己长期积累的相马的知识和经验，编写了一本《相马经》。书中配合文字还有插图，勾画出各种良马的形态和特点。

伯乐的儿子很想把父亲的专门技能继承下来，但他没有跟父亲学过相马。后来，他把《相马经》读得很熟，准备将来出去相马时，就根据书上所描绘的形态和特点去辨认识别好马。

伯乐的儿子自以为学到了识别良马的技术，便独自外出去寻找千里马。由于他没有实际知识和经验，只是按书本生搬硬套。虽然走了好多地方，遇见很多马匹，但也没有找到好马。

有一天，他走到一条小溪旁边，看见一只大蟾蜍。低头仔细一看，"啊！有了，有了！"他高兴地说。他想：《相马经》说千里马是"额角突出，眼睛闪光，四肢蹄大，大而端正"。这蟾蜍额头高高，眼睛突出发亮，蹼脚又很大，这与书上说的、画的千里马的样子是多么相似啊。于是，他连忙捉住那只蟾蜍，马上赶回家。

"爸爸，我找到千里马啦！"伯乐的儿子到家后，非常兴奋地对伯乐说："您看，它同书上的千里马一样，只是脚有些不太像。"

伯乐一看，真是哭笑不得，这不是蟾蜍吗。自己的儿子竟然这么蠢笨！伯乐冷笑着说：

"你找到的这匹千里马，不能跑只能跳，也不能骑啊！"

人们根据这个笑话引申出"按图索骥"这句成语，本来是讽刺那些不动脑筋，不会运用书本知识的人。现在比喻按照自己的线索去寻找所需要的东西。

In ancient times there lived in the State of Qin a man named Bo Le who was famous for being a connoisseur of fine horses. Over several decades, he had dealt with many thousands of horses. When Bo Le reached his elder years he compiled, based on his many years of experience, a book entitled "The Appraisal of Horses." In addition to a text, the book also contained illustrations and outlines of the forms and characteristics of every kind of horses.

Bo Le's son very much wanted to inherit his father's expertise and skills, but he never took the time to study the art of viewing and judging horses with his father. Later, he thoroughly read "The Appraisal of Horses," thinking he would try his hand at discerning fine horses based on the descriptions in the book.

When Bo Le's son felt he had attained the skill of appraising fine horses, he set off on his own in search of a "thousand-mile horse," a Chinese saying for a steed of exceptional quality. Because he had no practical experience or knowledge, he could only go mechanically by what was said in the book. Although he traveled to many places and came across many horses, he hadn't found any of quality.

One day, he came to a small brook and spotted a large toad there. Lowering his head for a closer look, he euphorically exclaimed, "Aha! I've found one!" He was thinking of the description of a thousand-mile horse in the book "The Appraisal of Horses": "A pronounced frontal eminence, glittering eyes, four hooves of a large size, and a large and upright bearing." This toad had a high forehead, bright and protruding eyes, and huge webbed feet. How much this resembled the thousand-mile horse described in the book! At this, he hurriedly caught the toad and immediately set off for home.

"Father, father! I found a thousand-mile horse!" Upon entering the house full of excitement, he said to Bo Le, "Please

3

look father, it's the same as the thousand-mile horse in the book, except that the feet are a bit different."

Bo Le didn't know whether to cry or laugh, because of course this was just a toad. How stupid was his own son! Bo Le smiled wryly and said, "This thousand-mile horse of yours cannot run, only hop. Who could possibly ride it?"

The idiom "look for a steed based on its picture" was based on this anecdote, and originally was meant to poke fun at those who don't use common sense or are unable to apply bookish knowledge. Today it is a metaphor for searching for something one wants based on a clue.

拔 苗 助 长

bá　miáo　zhù　zhǎng

（拔，pull upward；苗，shoot；助，help；长，grow）

HELP SHOOTS GROW
BY PULLING THEM UPWARD

传说，从前有一个农夫，是个急性子的人。每天他总是起早睡晚，辛勤地劳动，但总嫌田里的禾苗长得太慢。他希望能长得快些，今天去量量、明天又去量量，可是一天、两天、三天，他总感觉禾苗好象一点儿也没有长高，心中十分着急。

他一直在想，怎么能帮助禾苗长高呢？一天早晨，他终于想出了一个帮助禾苗生长快的"好办法"了。

他赶快到田里，头顶着炎炎的烈日把禾苗一棵一棵地往上拔高。从早晨干到中午，又从中午拔到太阳快要落山，把田里的禾苗一棵棵全都拔了一遍。他费了不少力气，累得腰酸腿痛，精疲力竭，可是，他心里非常高兴，以为这办法非常高明。

他拖着疲惫的双腿，摇摇晃晃回到家里，顾不得擦干身上的汗水，兴奋地告诉家人：

"今天可把我累坏了！地里这些禾苗不爱长，我帮助它们长高了好多啦！"

说完，他得意地坐在那里，拿起一把破扇子扇了起来。

他的儿子听了不明白是怎么回事，马上跑到田里去看，发现田里的禾苗全都枯萎了、死了。

人们根据这个寓言故事引申出"拔苗助长"这句成语，比喻不顾客观规律，急于求成，反将事情办槽了。

Once there was a farmer of an impatient disposition. Every day he awoke early, toiled and labored all day, and went to bed late, yet was always worried that his seedlings were growing too slowly. He hoped they would grow a bit faster, and would go out every day to measure their progress. But day after day it seemed to him that the shoots were not getting any taller, and this only made him more anxious.

He kept thinking to himself: How can I help the shoots grow? One morning, he finally hit upon a "great idea" for aiding the growth of his seedlings.

He rushed out to his fields, and with the blazing sun beating down on his head, proceeded to pull the seedlings one by one up higher. Working from morning to noon, and again from noon to dusk, he pulled up each and every shoot in his fields. His waist and legs were sore and tired, and he was totally worn out with effort, yet his heart was glad, because he considered his plan to be extremely clever.

Dragging his two exhausted legs, he staggered back home, and not even bothering to wipe the sweat from his body excitedly told his family, "Today really wore me out! I helped those stubborn little shoots grow a good deal!"

This said, he smugly sat down and began fanning himself with a raggedy old fan.

His son didn't understand what his father meant, and ran out to the fields to take a look, where he discovered all the shoots withered and dead.

The idiom "help shoots grow by pulling them upward" is drawn from this fable and refers to a situation where, by not taking into consideration objective reality and impatiently seeking results, the opposite of what one intended is achieved.

百 发 百 中

bǎi fā bǎi zhòng

(百, hundred; 发, shot; 中, hit the bull's eye)

A HUNDRED SHOTS,
A HUNDRED BULL'S – EYES

古时候，楚国有一个射箭能手名叫养由基。有一年，楚国与晋国打仗，养由基跟随楚国国王参加战斗。一次，在战场上，楚王被晋国一员大将射伤，当时楚王给养由基两支箭，要他射晋国大将。只见养由基张弓搭箭，一箭就把那人射死了。

养由基的射箭技术很高超，站在一百步以外的地方，对着只有三、四分宽，一寸左右长的柳叶射，一百支箭，射一箭，中一箭，百发百中。

养由基在楚国的名气很大，不少弓箭手都来向他请教射箭技艺。有一次，他又表演射箭，很多人都来看他百步穿杨、百发百中的精彩表演。他是张弓搭箭，指哪射哪，做到箭无虚发，围观的人都给他喝彩叫好。

正在他兴趣正浓，十分得意时，忽然听见有人说：

"还需教教他。"

养由基收了弓箭，就冲着那人走去，见是一位老人。他便以责问的口气说：

"难道你认为我的射箭技术不够高明吗？还要教教我吗？"

老人很平静地对他说：

"你的射箭本领确实很高明，我是没有本领教你如何拉弓射箭。我只是提醒你，你射箭时间长了，身体疲劳了，一旦你的气力不够，只要一箭没有射中，那你的百发百中的名声就要受到影响了，这不是前功尽弃了吗？"

养由基开始还有些傲慢、不高兴，听老人这么指点，确实是在教他，所以，对这位老人十分感激。

人们根据这个故事引申出"百发百中"这句成语，这个故事的前半部分是形容射箭技术的高超，也比喻预料事情很有把握。

In ancient times, a marksman by the name of Yang Youji lived in the State of Chu. One year, the states of Chu and Jin went to war with each other, and Yang Youji accompanied the Chu king to battle. One time on the battlefield, the Chu king was wounded by an arrow shot by a Jin general. The Chu king gave two arrows to Yang Youji in order to shoot the Jin general. Drawing his bow and cocking an arrow, Yang Youji shot the Jin general dead with one shot.

The skill of Yang Youji with the bow was exceptional. Standing at more than a hundred paces away, he could aim at a willow leaf half an inch wide and an inch and a half long, loose one hundred arrows in a row, and strike home each time.

Yang Youji was renowned throughout the State of Chu. Many marksmen came to him seeking instruction in archery techniques. One time he gave another exhibition, with many people coming to watch him put arrows through targets with great precision. Cocking arrows, he shot wherever he was pointed, and no arrow was shot in vain, much to the delight and cheering of the crowds.

At the height of his performance, when he was feeling the most confident, he suddenly heard someone say, "He still needs a bit of instruction."

Yang Youji put down his bow and arrows and strode over to the speaker, who was an old man, and said haughtily, "You think my technique with the bow is not good enough? Perhaps then you can teach me something?"

The old man replied levelly, "Your skill at shooting is indeed quite astounding, and I myself, having no such talent, have nothing to teach you concerning this. I only want to remind you, you've been shooting for a long time here and are growing tired. Should your strength falter and one shaft misses its mark, then your reputation for unfailing accuracy will suffer. Wouldn't that put at risk all you have worked for?"

At first Yang Youji was a bit put off, but in listening to the old man's advice, he did in fact learn something, and was thus grateful to the old man.

The idiom "a hundred shots, a hundred bull's-eyes" was drawn from this story, referring to the descriptions of excellent marksmanship, and can also refer to great accuracy in predicting situations.

杯 弓 蛇 影

bēi　　gōng　　shé　　yǐng

（杯，cup；弓，bow；蛇，snake；影，reflection）

MISTAKE THE REFLECTION OF A BOW
IN THE CUP FOR A SNAKE

从前有一个人，名叫乐广，很喜欢结交朋友，并经常邀请朋友到家里喝酒聊天。

　　有一天，他又请一位朋友到家里喝酒。两个人一边喝酒，一边谈话，二人都很高兴。这位朋友喝着、说着，突然间停止喝酒，马上告别回家了。乐广心里很纳闷，他为什么突然不喝酒就走了呢？

　　过了好几天，乐广一直没有见到这位朋友。就派家人去探望，这才知道，这位朋友生病了。为此，乐广亲自登门去看望，见他病得很厉害，便问：

　　"前几天我们在一起喝酒，你还好好的，怎么一下子就病倒了呢？"

　　开始这位朋友支支吾吾地不说。乐广问的紧了，这位朋友才说出实情：

　　"首先，谢谢您那天盛情招待我喝酒。我喝了几杯以后，突然间发现我的酒杯里有一条蛇，在杯中隐隐约约地，慢慢地蠕动，顿时很害怕，也很恶心。回家后全身都不舒服，总觉得肚子里有一条小蛇。就这样，我生病起不了床啦。"

　　乐广在回家的路上，心想：酒杯里怎么会有蛇呢？他坐在上次朋友喝酒时坐的凳子上，前面放只酒杯，果然见到杯中有一条蛇的影子。经过他细心观察，终于找到了原因。乐广立刻将这位朋友再次请到家中，扶他又坐在上次喝酒的地方，又请他喝酒。这位朋友非常不安，连连摆手说：

　　"我不喝，我不喝。"

　　乐广给他斟满一杯酒说：

　　"你看看酒杯中有什么？"

　　这位朋友心情特别紧张地说：

　　"同上次一样，杯中有蛇。"

　　这时，乐广指着墙上挂着的弓，说：

　　"都是它在作怪，杯中的蛇是这张弓的影子！"

　　随后，乐广把墙上的弓取下来，杯中的小蛇果然没有了。

　　这位朋友恍然大悟，便说：

"啊，原来如此，杯中的蛇是墙上弓的影子啊！"

顿时，消除了恐惧和疑惑，一下子病就全好了。

人们根据这个故事引申出"杯弓蛇影"这句成语，比喻因为疑神疑鬼而造成的一场虚惊。

Once there was a man named Yue Guang who loved to socialize, often inviting friends over to drink wine and chat.

One day he invited a friend over for a drink. The two drank wine and talked, enjoying themselves. All of a sudden, this friend stopped drinking and quickly bidding good-bye, left for home. Yue Guang puzzled, why did he suddenly stop drinking and leave?

Many days passed during which Yue Guang did not see his friend again. Dispatching a servant to ask around, he found out that his friend was ill. At this, Yue Guang went in person to pay a visit. Upon seeing that his friend's condition was very serious, he asked him, "A few days ago we drank together and you were in excellent health. How is it that you have now come down with illness?"

At first the friend just equivocated, not answering the question. When Yue Guang pressed however, the friend came out with the truth:

"First, thank you for your great hospitality in inviting me to drink with you that day. After I had finished several cups, I suddenly discovered a snake in my glass, indistinct but squirming around. I was immediately frightened, as well as nauseated. After returning home, my whole body was uncomfortable, and I felt as though my stomach held a small snake. So there it is, I've fallen sick and bedridden."

On the way home, Yue Guang thought to himself: How could there have been a snake in his wine glass?

After arriving home, Yue Guang came to the place where he and his friend drank together that day. He seated himself upon the stool where his friend drank, and placed a glass of wine before him. Sure enough, he saw the shape of a snake in the glass! After closer inspection, he finally discovered the reason. Yue Guang immediately invited his friend over, helped him into the seat where he drank before, and asked him to have a drink. The friend was extremely ill at ease, and waved his hands, saying, "No thanks, no thanks."

Yue Guang poured him a cup of wine and said, "Look in the cup, what do you see?"

Extremely unsettled, the friend replied, "The same as last time, there's a snake in the cup."

At this point, Yue Guang pointed to a bow hanging on the wall, and said, "There's the cause of this mischief, the snake is just the reflection of the bow in the glass!"

Yue Guang then took the bow down from the wall, at which the little snake in the glass disappeared.

Suddenly understanding, the friend became cheery, saying, "So that's what it was! Just the reflection of the bow!"

At once his fear and uncertainty were removed, and his illness cured.

The idiom "mistake the reflection of a bow in the cup for a snake" arose from this story as a metaphor for excessive suspicion or fear which results in a false alarm.

伯 乐 识 马

bó　　lè　　shí　　mǎ

(伯乐, name of a celestial being; 识, be good at judging; 马, horse)

BO LE JUDGES HORSES

神话中掌管天马的星神名叫伯乐，他能识别马的优劣好坏，特别能辨认和挑选千里马。

春秋时期，秦国有个名叫孙阳的人，他也能识别马的优劣好坏，是个著名的"相马"专家，人们表示对他的尊敬，就也称他为伯乐。

有一天，伯乐坐车到一个地方去，在半路上看见一匹很瘦的老马在拉车，车上装满了盐。它吃力地慢慢地行走着，尾巴无力地往下垂，蹄子上的铁马掌也磨掉了，浑身冒着汗，口水不时从嘴里流出来。盐车拉到半坡上，老马气喘吁吁，费力地拉着，实在走不动了，车夫不得不让它停下来歇息。

伯乐在路上注意了这匹老马，凭着他的眼力，认出了这是一匹难得的千里马。

伯乐看到优良的好马竟被用来拉盐车，还累成这个样子，很是痛心和惋惜。他赶忙从车上跳下来，走近千里马，亲切地抚摸着它的毛，并脱下自己的外衣披在马背上。

赶车人以奇怪的眼光看着伯乐的一举一动，心想：他怎么这样心疼这匹老马呢？

伯乐转过头来，问车夫：

"你怎能让它干活呢？"

车夫很坦然地说：

"马就是拉车的，盐啦……什么东西都拉。看来，你很心疼它呢？"

伯乐感叹地说：

"你可能不知道，这是一匹良马，是一匹能奔跑的好马，它能日行千里呢！这么好的马，用它拉沉重的盐太可惜了。让我怎么能不难过呢！"

这匹马也好像明白伯乐是爱护它、心疼它，把头依偎在伯乐的怀里，又不停地点着头。过一会，它仰起头，伸着脖子，朝天长嘶一声，仿佛在说：

"总算有人认出我是千里马了。"

伯乐为减轻这匹马的负担，将车上的盐卸下一部分，放在自

18

己的车上，一起把盐拉到目的地。 最后，伯乐付一笔钱，将马买下来了。 经过一阵精心喂养，这匹马果然能日行千里了。

后来人们根据这个故事引申出"伯乐识马"这句成语，比喻善于发现人材、识别人材，爱惜人材。

In mythology, the celestial being Bo Le appears as the caretaker of heavenly steeds. His skill at judging horses was exceptional, and he was especially able to select "thousand-mile horses," that is, horses of great strength and stamina.

During the Spring and Autumn Period, the State of Qin had a man named Sun Yang who was famous for his ability to discern the quality of horses. To express their respect for him, people called him Bo Le.

One day Bo Le was riding a chariot somewhere when he spied a thin horse pulling a cart laden with salt. Straining, the horse moved slowly forward, its tail hanging listlessly down, its shoes worn off, body frothing in sweat, and its saliva occasionally dripping out. The salt cart made it halfway up a hill, the old horse panting and panting, straining to pull the cart, which refused to budge any more. The cart master did not allow the horse to stop and rest.

From the street, Bo Le's attention was caught by this old horse, his judgment telling him that this was a rare thousand-mile steed.

Bo Le was both aggrieved and regretful when he saw how such a fine horse was being used to lug a salt cart, exhausted to its present condition. He quickly jumped down from his cart and approached the thousand-mile horse, fondly stroking its hide, and stripping off his own outer garment to lay across the horse's back.

The cart driver watched Bo Le's every movement with a curious eye, thinking to himself: How can he have so much affection for an old nag?

Turning his head, Bo Le spoke to the cart master, "How can you make him do hard labor?"

The cart master replied calmly, "Horses are for pulling carts, like salt ... or anything, really. It seems you're rather fond of him, yes?"

Sighing with emotion, Bo Le said, "You might not know, but this is a fine horse, a horse that can run, a horse that could run a thousand miles in a single day! Such a fine beast being used to lug heavy salt is a shame. How could I not be distressed!"

The horse appeared to understand Bo Le's care and affection for him and, placing his head in Bo Le's bosom, unceasingly nodded his head up and down. After a moment, he raised his head, extended his neck, and let out a long neigh towards heaven, as if to say, "At last, someone who can tell I am a thousand-mile steed!"

To relieve a bit of the horse's burden, Bo Le took some of the salt off the cart, placing it on his own, helping to carry it to its destination. Finally, Bo Le handed over a sum of money and purchased the horse. After a period of careful nurturing, the horse did indeed prove to be a thousand-mile horse.

Later, people used the idiom "Bo Le judges horses" to mean one who was good at discovering or judging, or who could appreciate, human ability.

唇 亡 齿 寒

chún wáng chǐ hán

(唇, lips; 亡, lose; 齿, teeth; 寒, cold)

IF THE LIPS ARE GONE,
THE TEETH WILL BE COLD

春秋初期，晋国是一个大国，它把周围的鼓、霍、耿等小国都灭掉了。

有一年，晋国想吞并在南面的小国虢（音 guó）国。但是，晋国出兵侵略虢国，必须要经过虞国的领土，这就需要向虞国借一条路。晋国为了能从虞国借路，还特意给虞国国君送去宝石和好马。虞国国君想到晋国是个大国，不敢得罪，况且自己也很喜爱这些礼物，因此，他想答应借路。

虞国有位大臣名叫宫之奇，他看穿了这次晋国出兵的阴谋，就急忙去见国君，劝他不要答应晋国借路的要求，他说：

"国君您还记得吧，前两年，晋国也是去打虢国，我们借路给他。那次晋国没有灭掉虢国，回师经过我国时，顺手牵羊，侵占了我们的一片土地。现在，晋国又要耍这套把戏。我们可不能再上当了，要吸取教训。"

国君自信地说：

"晋国国君和我是同姓宗族。他怎么能骗我呢？"

宫之奇反驳说：

"虢国也是晋国的同姓宗族，它怎么还去打它呢？"

国君还是不动声色，宫之奇继续说：

"我国和虢国紧紧连在一起，就好像嘴唇和牙齿互相依存一样。俗话说，'唇亡齿寒'，如果嘴唇没有了，牙齿就要寒冷了。虢国是我国的屏障，如果晋国灭了虢国，我国就孤单了，晋国随后就要侵略我们。所以，虢、虞两国，应当紧密团结相互支持，千万别借路给晋国。"

可是，虞国国君听后很不耐烦，说：

"你不要说了，这事由我来定，你回去吧。"

宫之奇已看出，国君不会听信他的劝告，预感到虞国要大祸临头了，便带着自己一家人逃走了。临走时说：

"可悲啊，虞国保不住了。"

晋国借路通过虞国，很快把虢国消灭了。在晋国得胜回国时，借口要在虞国休整几日，便来个突然袭击，又把虞国也消灭掉了。虞国国君成了俘虏。这时，他后悔已经晚了。

后来人们根据这个故事引申出"唇亡齿寒"这句成语，比喻互相依存，利害关系十分密切。

At the beginning of the Spring and Autumn Period, the State of Jin was a large kingdom which had wiped out the surrounding smaller states of Gu, Huo, and Geng.

One year, the State of Jin wanted to annex the smaller southern State of Guo. However, in order for Jin troops to be able to attack Guo, they had to pass through the territory of Yu. In order to gain passage through Yu, the king of Jin sent special gifts of precious stones and fine horses to the king of Yu. The Yu king thought that Jin was a pretty big state, he wouldn't want to offend it, and besides, he really liked these gifts. And so he decided to agree to allow the Jin army to pass through his country.

A minister of Yu named Gong Zhiqi saw through the plot by the State of Jin and hurriedly went to see the king. Advising him not to let the Jin march through Yu, he said, "If Your Majesty will recall, two years ago the Jin struck at Guo, and used our roads to do so. That time Jin did not eliminate Guo, and as they returned through our country, they occupied our lands at their convenience. Now, Jin wants to play this trick again. We must not be taken in again, we need to learn a lesson."

The king was confident. "The king of Jin and I are of the same clan. How could he deceive me?"

Gong Zhiqi countered with, "The king of Guo is also a clansman of the king of Jin, yet how can Jin attack Guo?"

The king remained unperturbed. Gong Zhiqi continued, "We and the State of Guo are closely involved with one another, as if we were lips and teeth. A common saying says, 'If the lips are gone, the teeth will be cold.' The State of Guo provides a protective screen for Yu. If Jin destroys Guo, Yu will be left all alone, and will sooner or later be invaded. Therefore, Guo and Yu should unite in mutual support. The Jin army must not pass through Yu."

But the king of Yu became impatient, saying, "There's nothing you need to say. This decision is mine. You will leave now."

24

Gong Zhiqi could already see that the king was not going to listen to his advice. Sensing that Yu was on the brink of disaster, he fled with his family. Just before leaving, he said, "How tragic that Yu cannot be saved."

Passing through Yu, the Jin quickly destroyed the State of Guo. Returning victorious, the Jin army used an excuse to rest and recuperate for a few days in Yu, and in a surprise attack, the Jin army wiped out Yu as well. The king of Yu became a prisoner of war, but by this time, his regret was too late.

Now the idiom "if the lips are gone, the teeth will be cold" has come to refer to a situation of interdependence and close relations of mutual benefit and harm.

此 地 无 银 三 百 两

cǐ dì wú yín sān bǎi liǎng

(此, this; 地, place; 无, no; 银, silver;
三, three; 百, hundred; 两, tael)

NO 300 TAELS OF SILVER BURIED HERE

从前有个人名叫张三，喜欢自作聪明。他积攒了三百两银子，心里很高兴，但是，他又很苦恼，怕这么多钱被别人偷走，不知存放在哪里才安全。带在身上吧，很不方便，容易让小偷察觉；放在抽屉里吧，觉得不妥当，也容易让小偷偷去；锁在箱子里吧，又怕小偷把银子和箱子一起偷走，也不保险。

　　他捧着三百两银子，苦思冥想了半天，想来想去，最后终于想出了自以为最好的办法。

　　张三趁黑夜，在自家房后墙角下挖了一个坑，悄悄地把银子埋在里边。埋好后，他还是不放心，害怕别人怀疑这里埋了银子。他想了又想，终于又想出一个自以为绝妙的办法。他回屋，在一张白纸上写上"此地无银三百两"七个大字。然后，出去贴在坑边的墙上。他感到这样是很安全了，便回屋睡觉了。

　　张三一整天心神不定的样子，早已被邻居王二注意到了，晚上王二又听到屋外有挖坑的声音，感到奇怪。就在张三回屋睡觉时，王二去了屋后，借月光，看见墙角上贴着纸条，写着"此地无银三百两"七个大字。王二一切都明白了。他轻手轻脚地把银子扒出来，再把坑填好。

　　王二回到家里，见到眼前白花花的银子高兴极啦，但又害怕起来。他想，如果明天张三发现银子丢了，怀疑是我偷走的怎么办？于是，他也灵机一动，自作聪明地拿起笔，在纸上写道"隔壁王二不曾偷"七个大字，也贴在坑边的墙角上。

　　后来人们根据这个民间故事，把这两句话"此地无银三百两，隔壁王二不曾偷"当做一个成语了，用来比喻自作聪明，想要隐瞒、掩饰所干的事情，结果反而更加暴露明显了。

　　现在这句成语，被简化为"此地无银三百两"了。

There once lived a man named Zhang San who loved to think himself clever. Bit by bit, he had collected 300 taels of silver, which delighted him. But he was also worried that so much silver would be stolen, and couldn't figure out a safe place to keep it. Keeping it on his person would be inconvenient and easily observed by thieves; putting it in a drawer wouldn't be right either, and could also be stolen easily; he could lock it in a chest, but a thief could just take the chest and the silver.

Scooping up the silver, he puzzled for a long time, mulling the problem over. Finally, he hit upon what he considered to be the best idea.

Working under the cover of darkness, he dug a pit in a corner of the wall behind his house, and stealthily buried the silver there. Afterwards, he still felt uneasy, afraid that someone may suspect that the silver was buried there. He thought and thought, and came up again what he thought was an ingenious solution. Returning to his room, he took a large sheet of white paper and wrote on it in large characters: No 300 taels of silver buried here. Then, he went out and pasted it on the wall above the spot where the silver was buried. Feeling safe at last, he went back inside and went to sleep.

Zhang San's uneasiness throughout the day has aroused the attention of his neighbor, Wang Er, who at night heard the sound of digging outside and felt it strange. When Zhang San went to sleep, Wang Er went to the rear of the house, and by the light of the moon read the words written on the paper posted on the wall: No 300 taels of silver buried here. Wang Er understood at once. Soft of hand and foot, he dug the silver up, then filled the hole back in.

Wang Er returned home and was elated at the silver sparkling before his eyes. But he also became scared. He thought: What if tomorrow Zhang San discovers the silver is missing and suspects me? Suddenly inspired, he took up a brush and wrote seven large characters on a sheet of paper which he stuck on the wall above the pit: Neighbor Wang Er never stole the silver.

The two phrases from this story, "No 300 taels of silver buried here," and "Neighbor Wang Er never stole the silver," have been adopted to refer to someone who thinks they are being very clever in covering something up, but who in the end only makes things more obvious.

Now this idiom has been shortened to just the first phrase, "No 300 taels of silver buried here."

呆 若 木 鸡

dāi　rùo　mù　jī

（呆, dumb; 若, look like; 木, wooden; 鸡, chicken）

DUMB AS A WOODEN CHICKEN

古代春秋战国时，曾流行"斗鸡"，这是一种赌博性的娱乐活动。当时有一个叫纪渻（音 xǐng）子的人，就是有名的斗鸡专家。

有一天，齐王聘请纪渻子为他训练斗鸡。

刚训练十天，齐王便派人去询问：

"斗鸡训练成了吗？可以拿出去斗了吗？"

纪渻子说：

"不行，这只鸡一看见别的鸡，就把头昂得高高的，看上去气呼呼的样子，很不沉着，若是拿出去斗，一定要斗败的。"

又过了十天，齐王很着急，又派人去问道：

"这回斗鸡该训练得差不多了吧？"

纪渻子忙回答说：

"还是不行，这只鸡一见别的鸡，反应非常快，心神不定，若是拿出去斗，一定要失败的。"

再过了十天，齐王再次派人询问。

纪渻子说：

"这只鸡有进步，但还是不行。它的眼睛常转动，还不能克制，再训练几天吧。"

纪渻子训练这只鸡已经有四十天了，齐王亲自来看斗鸡。纪子告诉齐王：

"现在可以拿去斗鸡了。"

齐王非常高兴，马上拿去斗鸡。这场斗鸡吸引了很多人来观看。

纪渻子训练出来的这只鸡，在赛场上表现得心神很安定，骄气没有了，目不斜视地站立着。无论对手怎样鸣叫，它都不害怕，好像没有听到，毫无反应，看上去真像只木头做的鸡一样，不惊不动，所以，没有一个参赛的对手敢接近它；有的一见到它转身就逃跑了，更不敢同它斗了。

人们从故事里引申出"呆若木鸡"这句成语。原来是形容精神高度集中，后来用它形容人呆笨；也用它比喻因害怕或惊讶而发呆的样子。

In ancient times, during the Spring and Autumn and Warring States period, cock fighting was a popular form of gambling and entertainment. During that time there lived a man named Ji Xingzi who was an expert in the sport.

One day, the king of the State of Qi invited Ji Xingzi to train a fighting cock for him.

After ten days of training, the king sent someone to ask about the cock. "Has the bird completed its training yet? Is it ready to fight?"

"Not yet. As soon as this cock sees another bird, it holds its head up high, hisses, and loses its calm. Were it to compete now, it would surely lose," Ji Xingzi replied.

Another ten days passed, and the king became anxious, again sending someone to ask, "Is the cock's training almost completed?"

Ji Xingzi busily answered, "Still not yet. Its reactions are very fast upon seeing another rooster, and it becomes very uneasy. Were it to compete now, it would surely lose."

After another ten days, the king sent another person to inquire. Ji Xingzi said, "This cock has made progress, but it is still not yet ready. His eyes roll around too much, and it hasn't learned enough control. It requires a few more days of training."

When Ji Xingzi had had the cock under training for 40 days, the king of Qi himself came to see the fighting bird. Ji Xingzi told the king, "Now he is ready to fight."

The king was delighted, and immediately took the bird to fight. This bout attracted many spectators.

In the arena, this bird which Ji Xingzi had trained appeared totally unfazed, and stood immobile, eyes unstaring. No matter how his opponent cried or called, he remained unafraid and showed no reaction, as though he hadn't heard a thing. He seemed as though he were actually made out of wood. Therefore, none of his opponents dared to approach him; some, upon seeing him turn his body, would flee, and became even more scared to tangle with him.

The idiom "dumb as a wooden chicken" originally described a high degree of concentration, but later came to be used to describe stupidity in people. It is also used metaphorically to describe one who is struck dumb with fear, terror, or surprise.

道 听 途 说

dào　tīng　tú　shūo

(道, road; 听, hear; 途, way; 说, say)

HEARD ON THE STREETS
AND TOLD ON THE ROADS

从前，有一个名叫艾子的人，带着学生到城里去。在路上遇见了他的朋友毛空。

　　艾子问他："最近我没有出门，有什么新闻吗？"

　　毛空忙说："有有，有户人家的一只鸭子，一次生了一百个鸭蛋。"

　　艾子说："我不相信，这怎么可能呢？"

　　毛空改口说："那么是两只鸭子生的蛋。"

　　艾子说："这也不可能。"

　　毛空又改口说："那大概是三只鸭子生的蛋吧。"

　　艾子还是不相信。

　　毛空见艾子总是怀疑不相信，他就一次又一次地把鸭子的数目一直增加到了十只。

　　艾子问他："你为什么不减少鸭蛋数目呢？"

　　毛空说："我宁可增加鸭子的只数，也不能减少了我已经说出了的鸭蛋的数目。"

　　艾子心想，这个人真是爱说空话，也只好一笑了之。

　　毛空见艾子不相信他说的这件新闻，便又说："我还有一件新闻呢。"

　　艾子说："你再说说看。"

　　毛空说："上个月，天上掉下来一块肉，可真重啊！有三十丈长、十丈宽。"

　　艾子不相信，说："哪能有这种事，我可不信。"

　　毛空说："那就是二十丈长吧。"

　　艾子还是不相信。

　　毛空又改口说："大概是十丈吧。"

　　艾子说："就按你说的，是十丈长，天上能掉下来这么大块肉吗？你见到了吗？这块肉掉在什么地方？还有，刚才你说的那只鸭子是谁家养的呢？"

　　毛空支支吾吾地答不上来，只好承认，说："我是在路上听别人说的。"

　　于是，艾子对他的学生说："你们可不能像毛空那样道听途说啊！"

　　后来人们根据这个故事引申出"道听途说"这句成语，比喻没有事实根据或无中生有的传闻。

Once there was a man named Ai Zi who was taking his students into the city. On the road, he bumped into his friend Mao Kong.

"I haven't been out lately, has there been any news?" Ai Zi asked.

Mao Kong quickly replied, "Oh yes, yes. Someone's duck laid 100 eggs at a single time."

Ai Zi said, "I don't believe it. How is that possible?"

Mao Kong replied, "Then it was two ducks that laid the eggs."

"That's impossible, too," Ai Zi said.

Mao Kong spoke again, "Then it was probably three ducks."

Ai Zi still didn't believe the story.

Mao Kong saw that Ai Zi kept doubting the tale, and thus kept changing the number of ducks until their number reached ten.

Ai Zi asked him, "Why don't you reduce the number of eggs in the story?"

Mao Kong said, "I prefer to raise the number of ducks. Since I've already specified the number of eggs, I can't change that."

Ai Zi thought to himself: This guy really likes to blow hot air. Best to just laugh it off.

Seeing that Ai Zi didn't believe this tale, Mao Kong said, "I have another bit of news."

"Let's hear it," Ai Zi said.

"Last month, this huge chunk of meat fell from the sky! It had to have been about a hundred feet long, and thirty feet wide," Mao Kong said.

Unbelieving, Ai Zi said, "How could that be? I don't believe it."

"Then it was about sixty feet long," Mao Kong said.

Ai Zi still didn't believe the story.

Mao Kong said, "Then it was probably about thirty feet long."

Ai Zi said, "Let's say it was thirty feet long. Is it possible that such a big chunk of meat could fall from the sky? Did you see it? Where did this chunk of meat fall? And moreover, who did that duck you just spoke of belong to?"

Mao Kong hemmed and hawed for a moment, then finally admitted, "I heard it from someone else."

Thereupon, Ai Zi said to his students, "Don't you become like Mao Kong, paying attention to things heard on the streets and told on the roads!"

Now this idiom "heard on the streets and told on the roads" is used to describe rumors with no basis in reality or fabricated stories.

对 症 下 药

duì　zhèng　xià　yào

(对, on the basis of; 症, illness; 下, prescribe; 药, remedy)

SUIT THE REMEDY TO THE ILLNESS

在中国东汉末年,有个著名医生名叫华佗。他的医术非常高明。他在给人治病时,总是详细询问病情、患病的经过,并仔细观察,找出患病的原因。所以,他的诊断极为准确,再根据病症情况开出处方来。

有一次,一个叫李延、一个叫倪(音 ní)寻的两个人都患了头痛发热病,同时来找华佗治病。经过详细询问病情,细心诊断后,华佗给他两人各开了一个药方,李延要服发散药;而倪寻要吃泻药。两个人互相看了药方以后,感到很奇怪,问道:"我们两人都患一样的病,为什么用的药却不一样呢?"

华佗解释说:

"用药要看病人病情的具体情况。虽然你二人病症相同,但患病的原因却不同。李延的身体内部没有什么毛病,病是由于外部受凉、感冒引起的;而倪寻的身体外部没有什么毛病,病是因吃东西太多,伤食,由内部引起的。患病的原因不同,当然用药就不能相同了。"

李延和倪寻听后,便放心地各自服用不同的药,二人的病都很快医治好了。

后来人们根据这个故事引申出"对症下药"这句成语,比喻针对客观实际情况,采取相应的办法,妥善处理一些问题。

During the last years of the Eastern Han Dynasty, there lived a famous physician named Hua Tuo, whose skill with medicine was superb. When treating a patient, he would always make a detailed inquiry into the symptoms and progression of an illness, and, through careful observation, ascertain the causes of a disease. Therefore, his diagnoses were quite accurate, and treatments were prescribed on the basis of each illness.

One time, two men named Li Yan and Ni Xun both came to Hua Tuo suffering from headaches and fever. After detailed questioning and careful diagnosis, he prescribed treatments for the two men. Upon comparing the two prescriptions, the two men were puzzled, and asked, "The two of us are suffering from the same illness. Why are the medications you prescribed different?"

Hua Tuo replied, "Treatment depends on the specific circumstances of the patient. Although the two of you have similar illnesses, their causes are actually quite different. Li Yan has nothing wrong internally, but he has contracted a cold from external causes. Ni Xun has nothing wrong externally, but has become ill from excessive eating and drinking, an internal problem. With two different causes, of course the treatments will be different.

After hearing this explanation, Li Yan and Ni Xun were put at ease, and, taking their respective medicines, both men speedily recovered.

The idiom "suit the remedy to the illness" came out of this story. It is used as a metaphor for skillfully handling a problem in view of the practical situation by adopting suitable means.

对 牛 弹 琴

duì　niú　tán　qín

（对, toward; 牛, cow; 弹, play; 琴, zither）

PLAY THE ZITHER TO A COW

古时候，有一位著名音乐家名叫公明仪。他能作曲也能演奏，七弦琴弹得非常好，弹的曲子优美动听，很多人都喜欢听他弹琴，人们很敬重他。可是在其他事情上公明仪也曾闹出笑话来。

公明仪不但在室内弹琴，遇上好天气还喜欢带琴到郊外弹奏。有一天，他来到郊外，春风徐徐地吹着，垂柳轻轻地拂动着，一条黄牛正在草地上低头吃草。他一时兴致来了，摆上琴，拨动琴弦，就给老牛弹奏起来了。可是，老牛在那里却无动于衷，仍然低头一个劲地吃草。

他想，这支曲子可能太高雅了，我换个曲调，弹弹小曲。老牛仍然毫无反应，继续悠闲地吃草。

公明仪拿出自己的全部本领，弹奏最拿手的曲子。这回呢，老牛偶尔甩甩尾巴，赶着牛虻，仍然低头闷不吱声地吃草。

最后，老牛慢悠悠地走了。换个地方去吃草了。

公明仪见给老牛弹了很长时间的琴，而老牛始终无动于衷，很是失望，最后也只好叹口气，抱琴回去了。真是自找没趣。

后来人们根据这个故事引申出"对牛弹琴"这句成语，比喻对不懂道理的人讲道理，是白费口舌；也常用来讥笑说话不看对象的人。

In ancient times there was a famous musician named Gong Mingyi. Both a composer and a performer, he could play the zither exceptionally well. People were often moved by his playing, and he gained respect and admiration. But in other matters he was often known to make a fool of himself.

Gong Mingyi not only played indoors, but on days when the weather was fair, he liked to take his instrument to the countryside and play there. One day when he came to the countryside, a spring breeze was softly blowing, the drooping willows were gently swaying, and an ox was standing in a field, head lowered, munching grass. Stricken with the mood, he set up his zither and began plucking away in a performance for the ox. The old ox, however, remained indifferent, still intent on eating grass.

Gong Mingyi thought to himself, "Perhaps this tune is a bit too refined, perhaps I should play a popular little ditty." The ox still showed no reaction. It just continued to stand there, leisurely munching away.

Mustering all of his skill, Gong Mingyi began playing his best tune. At this, the ox swished his tail, shooing away flies, and continued silently eating grass.

Finally, the old ox ambled away in search of another patch of grass.

Gong Mingyi felt disappointed when he saw the old ox's indifference to his performance. In the end he just sighed, picked up his instrument, and went home.

Later, the idiom "play the zither to a cow" arose out of this story. It is used for instance when wasting one's breath trying to reason with an unreasonable person, or as a term of derision for those who speak yet don't keep in mind their audience.

负 荆 请 罪

fù　jīng　qǐng　zùi

（负，carry；荆，birch；请罪，admit one's error and ask for punishment）

PROFFER A BIRCH AND ASK FOR A FLOGGING

战国时期，赵国有一名叫蔺（音 lìn）相如的大臣。他很机灵，并有胆量。当时秦国很强大，而赵国比较弱小。秦王总想欺负赵国。蔺相如曾冒着生命危险，聪明而又巧妙地同秦王进行了坚决斗争，使赵国免受损失，为此他为赵国立了大功。赵王很重用蔺相如，把他提升为赵国最高的官位——上卿。

当时，赵国还有一名老将军叫廉颇，他是有功之臣，为赵国立了很大功劳，因此他很骄傲。他对提升蔺相如很不满意、不服气，并对别人说：

"我作为赵国的大将军，历年来在战场上出生入死，为国家立了多少功劳。他蔺相如算老几，只靠会说话，就立功了，官位比我还高，怎能让人忍受得了。我实在感到没脸见人了。"还扬言：

"我要是遇见了蔺相如，一定要给他点颜色看不可！"

蔺相如知道了这些情况后，尽量不与廉颇见面，减少磨擦，处处忍让。每逢国王有事要召见所有大臣时，蔺相如就托称有病请假，有意不与廉颇见面。

蔺相如身边的人，都说他太胆小、太软弱了，感到羞惭，纷纷要求离开他。蔺相如挽留他们，说：

"各位比比看，廉颇将军和秦王两人哪个厉害？"

大家说："当然是秦王了。"

"秦王那么威风、那么厉害，我都敢在文武百官面前斥责他，难道我单单怕廉颇将军。"

"那么你为什么对廉将军总是躲躲闪闪的呢？"大家问他。

蔺相如说：

"我是考虑强大的秦国不敢侵略我们赵国，就是因为我们的文武百官能同心协力，团结一致。如果我与廉将军不和，如同两只老虎相斗，最后是两败俱伤，这对秦国是有利的。我之所以这样做，是因为首先考虑到国家的安危，才不计较个人的恩恩怨怨。"

这一番话，传到廉颇那里。老将军想到以前自己的言行深感不对，很是渐愧。于是，为了表示自己认错的诚意，他光着上身，背着荆条，来到蔺相如家里，跪在地上，向蔺相如请罪，并说：

"我是个粗鲁的人，不知道您是如此宽宏大量，请您用荆条抽打我吧！"

蔺相如连忙将廉颇扶起来，从此二人成为亲密朋友。

人们从这个故事引申出"负荆请罪"这句成语，表示主动向别人认错、道歉的意思。

During the Warring States Period, the State of Zhao had a minister named Lin Xiangru who was both intelligent and bold. At that time, the State of Qin was very powerful, while Zhao was relatively weak. The king of Qin was always finding ways to bully Zhao. Lin Xiangru had once risked mortal danger by engaging the king of Qin in a decisive battle of words and had prevented Zhao from taking any losses. Thusly had he performed a great service to the State of Zhao. The king of Zhao was very impressed and elevated Lin Xiangru to the highest ministerial post in the country.

At that time there was another talented minister in Zhao named Lian Po, who was a former general. Having performed many meritorious deeds for his country, he was quite proud. He was unhappy and resentful of Lin Xiangru's promotion, saying to others, "I was a great general and risked my life on the battlefield many times over the years. I've contributed much to my country. Who does this Lin Xiangru think he is? His great deeds depend on nothing but the ability to talk, yet his post is higher than mine. How can that be tolerated? I have truly lost face."

He also threatened, "If I ever run into him, I'll teach him a thing or two!"

When Lin Xiangru became aware of this situation, he did everything he could to avoid contact with Lian Po, hoping that an exercise in forbearance could reduce friction between the two. Every time the king would call his ministers together for a meeting, Lin Xiangru would claim illness, excusing himself so as not to have to confront Lian Po.

Those around Lin Xiangru began to be embarrassed by him, saying he was cowardly and weak. Gradually, people began to disassociate themselves from Lin Xiangru. He urged people to remain, saying, "Please think it over. Of Lian Po and the king of Qin, who is the more fierce?"

Everyone answered, "The king of Qin, of course."

"The king of Qin is so mighty and terrible, yet I reproached him in front of all his civil and military ministers. What do I have to fear from General Lian Po?"

"Then why are you always avoiding General Lian Po?" everyone asked.

Lin Xiangru replied, "I am thinking that the reason why Qin does not dare invade our country is because all our officials are of one mind and heart. If there is discord between General Lian Po and I, it will be as two tigers fighting. In the end no one wins except the State of Qin. Thus have I acted, placing consideration for the nation over my personal feelings."

When these words made it to Lian Po's ears, the former general was ashamed, feeling that his words and actions were deeply mistaken. Therefore, in order to express sincere recognition of his error, he stripped his torso and approached Lin Xiangru carrying birches. Kneeling, he pleaded for punishment, saying, "I am a crude and boorish person who did not know your great capacity for tolerance. Please take these birches and whip me!"

Lin Xiangru hurriedly helped Lian Po to his feet, and from this point on the two men became fast friends.

The idiom "proffer a birch and ask for a flogging" is used to indicate one who acknowledges his error to another and makes an apology.

邯 郸 学 步

hán dān xué bù

(邯郸, a city in present Hebei province;
学, learn; 步, way of walking)

LEARN THE HANDAN WAY OF WALKING

战国时期，赵国都城邯郸这个地方的人，走起路来姿势很优美，步子很轻快，手脚的摆动也非常别致。邯郸人会走路是远近闻名的。

燕国有一个年轻人，他嫌燕国人走路的样子不好看，姿势不优美、太土气。听说赵国邯郸人会走路，很是羡慕，就下定决心，到邯郸去，学走路。

这个年轻人走了很远的路，吃了不少苦头，终于到了邯郸。他一走进城里，见很多人来来往往的，觉得这里的人走路的样子与其他地方就是不一样，一伸手、一抬腿都很有风度，走路的姿势就是好看，真是名不虚传。

这个年轻人心想，若是我走路也象这个样子，回家后，大家也一定会羡慕我的。于是，他整天在街道旁，细心地观察邯郸人走路。

几天后，他也开始模仿人家走路了，但是学来的姿势总感到别扭，走起路来很不自然。

他又想，怎么学不象呢？可能是自己走了这么多年的路，都已经习惯了。要学新的走路姿势，必须改掉原来的习惯走法，从头学起。于是，他一步一步走着、学着，走一步的长短距离、手脚摆动、腰部姿势都按邯郸人的尺寸、步法去做。

这个年轻人学了很长时间，学得很吃力，结果呢？始终没有学会邯郸人走路的样子，反而把自己原来的走路步法也都忘掉了。他在邯郸住了几个月了，带的路费也全花光了，最后不得不回老家，可是，他已经忘掉自己是怎样走路的，只好爬着回去了。

根据这个故事引申出"邯郸学步"这句成语，比喻生搬硬套去模仿别人，反而会弄巧成拙，闹出笑话。

In the Warring States Period, people in Handan, the capital of the State of Zhao, walked with a posture of grace and beauty. Their steps were light and brisk, and movement of their hands and feet unique. The manner of walking of the Handan people was heard of far and wide.

In the State of Yan there lived a youth who disliked the way the people of Yan walked, feeling it to be ungainly and crude. Hearing how the people in Handan of Zhao walked, he was envious, and made up his mind to go to Handan to learn their way of walking.

The young man traveled a long distance and encountered many hardships before finally arriving in Handan. When he entered the city, he saw many people going about, and felt that the way they walked was indeed different than other places. The extension of a hand, the raising of a foot, all had a sense of high bearing. Their manner of walking was very seemly and indeed worthy of its reputation.

The youngster thought to himself, "If I also learn to walk this way, when I go home, everyone will certainly be envious of me." Therefore, he would spend all day on the roadside carefully observing the people of Handan walk.

After several days he began to imitate people's walking, but always did so awkwardly and unnaturally.

He thought to himself again, "Why can't I get it right? It might be possible that it's because I'm too accustomed to the way I've walked all these years. To learn a new manner of walking, I must lose my original manner and start from the beginning." Thus he began walking step-by-step, studying, taking a single step, swinging his arms, holding his back in imitation of the Handan people.

The young man practiced for a long time, putting in no small effort. And the result? He never was able to learn the Handan way of walking, and instead forgot his original way of walking. He lived in Handan for several months and spent all of his money, finally forcing him to go home. But, he had already forgotten how to walk, and was forced to crawl back home.

The idiom "learn the Handan way of walking," drawn from this story, is a metaphor for rote imitation of others, and in the attempt to be clever, make a fool of oneself.

囫 囵 吞 枣

hú　lún　tūn　zǎo

(囫囵, whole; 吞, swallow; 枣, date)

SWALLOW DATES WHOLE

传说从前有一个呆子，家中很有钱。有一次，他到市场上买了好多水果，有梨、苹果、枣等。这个呆子就坐在市场旁大吃起来。

他一会儿吃梨、一会儿吃枣，这样没完没了地吃着。正在他吃得高兴时，有一位医生从这里路过，见到这个呆子这样吃法，就对他说：

"梨可不能多吃，它虽然对牙齿有好处，但你吃多了会伤脾的。"

呆子听医生这么一说，就不再吃梨，而是一个接一个地吃枣。医生又说了：

"红枣虽然能补脾，对脾有好处，但吃多了对牙齿没有好处，会伤牙齿的，也不能多吃的。"

呆子听了医生这些话后，不知如何是好了，梨、枣……都不敢吃了。呆呆的坐在那里，过了一会，他兴奋地说：

"我有办法了！用这个办法，我既能吃梨，同时又能吃枣而且既不会伤脾，又不会伤牙齿。"

医生听他这么说，有些莫名其妙，就请他说出来。这个呆子自作聪明地说：

"吃梨的时候，只用牙齿咀嚼，而不咽到肚子里去，这样对牙齿有好处，又不会伤脾；而在吃枣时，我不用咀嚼，就一口吞下肚子里，这样可以不伤牙齿，又对脾有好处的。"

他说完，就把枣一个一个地扔在嘴里，不经过咀嚼，囫囵地吞下去了。过了一会，呆子的肚子就痛起来了。

医生见此情景，忙说：

"你这样把枣囫囵吞下去，肠胃不能消化和吸收，对脾也是没有好处的。"

后来人们根据这个故事引申出"囫囵吞枣"这句成语。比喻对所学、所用的东西不加分析、思考、不求消化理解而笼统地接受。

Once upon a time there was a slow-witted man who came from a very wealthy family. One time, he went to the market and bought a lot of fruit: pears, apples, dates, and other things. The simpleton then sat down by the market and proceeded to eat.

Alternately eating pears, then dates, he ate like this with no end in sight. As he was happily eating away, a physician passed by and, seeing how the fool was eating, said, "You shouldn't eat too many pears. Although they are good for the teeth, they can harm your spleen if you eat too many of them."

At this the dimwit stopped eating pears and began eating dates one after another. The physician said again, "Although dates can help your spleen, they're bad for your teeth if you eat too many."

After hearing this bit by the physician, the dunce didn't know what to do, not daring to eat either the pears or the dates. After sitting there stupefied for a moment he said excitedly, "I know, I can eat pears and dates at the same time. That way, it won't hurt my spleen or my teeth!"

The physician was a bit puzzled, and asked him to explain what he meant. Feeling himself to be quite clever, the dopey man answered, "When I eat a pear, I can just chew it with my teeth and not swallow it. This way, it will be good for my teeth and won't hurt my spleen. And when I eat a date, I won't chew it, I can just swallow it whole. This way it won't hurt my teeth, and it will be good for my spleen."

When he finished talking, he began popping dates into his mouth and swallowing them without chewing. After a moment, the simpleton's stomach began to ache fiercely.

When the physician saw this he hurriedly said, "When you swallow the dates whole, your intestines can't digest and absorb them. It doesn't do your spleen any good, either."

This story gave rise to the idiom "swallow dates whole," used to describe those who copy or use something without analysis, consideration, or understanding.

狐 假 虎 威

hú jiǎ hǔ wēi

(狐, fox; 假, borrow; 虎, tiger; 威, fierceness)

THE FOX BORROWS THE TIGER'S FIERCENESS

在森林里，有一只老虎正在寻找食物。忽然有一只狐狸从它身边窜过，老虎立刻猛扑过去，要吃掉狐狸。狡猾的狐狸一看，逃跑已经来不及了，便故作镇静地对老虎说：

"你怎么敢吃我呢！"

"我为什么不敢吃你？"老虎一愣神，问。

"我是老天爷派到森林里做兽王的，是来管理所有的野兽的。如果你把我吃了，就是违背了老天爷的命令。这对你是没有好处的。"

狐狸这么一说，老虎被它蒙骗住了，立刻松开了爪子。老虎看狐狸这么瘦小，就能当兽王了，实在有些不相信。狐狸看出了老虎的神色，便摇了摇尾巴说：

"你如果不相信，那么我带你在百兽面前走一趟，看看那些野兽见了我怕不怕。"

老虎同意了。

狐狸在前面走，老虎紧跟在后边，朝森林的深处走去。

森林里的黄羊、小鹿、兔子……看见狐狸昂着头，神气十足地走过来。大家都很纳闷，这只狐狸同往常怎么不一样呢？再往狐狸身后一看，呀！怎么狐狸后面跟着一只大老虎呢，这些野兽吓得都拼命逃跑了。

狐狸得意地对老虎说：

"你看见了吧，百兽们谁不怕我呢！"

其实，狡猾的狐狸是借着老虎的威风，把百兽吓跑了。

真正的百兽之王——老虎受骗了，它以为树林中的百兽果真怕狐狸呢。

后来人们根据这个动物故事引申出"狐假虎威"这句成语，比喻借助、倚仗别人的威势来欺压人、吓唬人。

A tiger was searching for food in the forest when suddenly a fox passed right in front of him. Immediately the tiger leapt, preparing to devour the fox. The crafty fox saw that it was too late to run, so, feigning an air of calmness, he said, "How dare you eat me!"

"Why shouldn't I eat you!" the tiger roared.

"I am the King of Beasts dispatched to the forest by Heaven to watch over all the wild beasts. If you eat me, it will violate the command of Heaven, and that won't do you any good."

The tiger was taken in by the fox's words, and immediately released him. Looking at the fox's thin, small body, the tiger was a little doubtful that he could really be the King of Beasts. Seeing the tiger's expression, the fox shook his tail and said, "If you don't believe me, come with me to visit the other animals and see if they are afraid of me or not."

The tiger agreed.

With the fox in front and the tiger following behind, they headed into the deep of the forest.

In the forest, gazelles, deer, and rabbits saw the fox, head held high, proudly approaching. All were puzzled — why was the fox acting so differently? Looking behind the fox — yikes! There was a tiger following the fox! All the wild animals ran for their lives.

The fox smugly said to the tiger, "See? Out of all the beasts, who is not afraid of me?"

Of course, the sly fox was only taking advantage of the ferocity of the tiger to frighten all the animals.

The true King of Beasts, the tiger, was duped, thinking that all the animals were really afraid of the fox.

Thus we have the idiom "the fox borrows the tiger's fierceness" to describe using or depending on another's power and influence to bully or frighten people.

画　蛇　添　足

huà　shé　tiān　zú

（画，draw；蛇，snake；添，add；足，feet）

DRAW A SNAKE AND ADD FEET TO IT

古时候，楚国有一家人，祭过了祖宗以后，便将祭祖用过的一壶酒，赏给手下的办事人员喝。

参加办事的人不少，这壶酒如果大家都喝是不够的，若是让一个人喝，那就能喝个痛快。这一壶酒到底给谁喝呢？

大家都安静下来，这时有人提议：每个人都在地上画一条蛇，谁画得快、又画得象，就把这壶酒给他喝。大家认为这个办法好，都同意这么办，于是，在地上画起蛇来。

有个人画得很快，一转眼最先画好了，就端起酒壶想要喝酒。但他回头看看别人，还都没有画好呢，心想：他们画得真慢。他想再显显自己的本事，于是，便左手提着酒壶，右手拿了一根树枝，给蛇画起脚来，还得意洋洋地说：

"你们画得好慢啊，我再给蛇画上几只脚也不算晚呢！"

正在他一边画着蛇脚，一边得意地说话的时候，另一个人已经把蛇画好了。那个人马上把酒壶从他手中夺过去，说：

"你看见过蛇吧？蛇是没有脚的，你为什么给它添上脚呢？画上脚就不是蛇了，所以，第一个画好蛇的应该是我，而不是你了。"

那个人说罢就仰起头来，理直气壮地，咕咚咕咚喝起酒来。

给蛇添足的那个人，无话可说，懊恼地看着别人把这壶酒喝了。

以后人们根据这个故事引申出"画蛇添足"这句成语，比喻有的人自作聪明，常作多余的事，节外生枝，反而弄巧成拙，把事情办糟了。

In ancient times, after performing rituals of ancestor worship, a family in the State of Chu gave a pot of ritual wine to the servants.

Because there were many servants, there wasn't enough wine to go around, though there was enough for one person to enjoy himself. The problem then arose of who should get the wine.

Everyone became quiet, until someone made a suggestion. Everyone would draw a snake on the ground. Whoever drew the snake the fastest and the best would get to drink the wine. Everyone agreed that this was a fine idea, and the drawing soon began.

One person drew very fast, completing a snake in the twinkling of an eye. Picking the wine jug up, he looked around at the others, who had yet to finish their drawings. He thought to himself, "They draw so slow!" Holding the wine in one hand and a pen in the other, he thought he would show off a bit, and drew some legs on the snake. Smugly, he said to the others, "You're so slow — I've already given the snake several feet and I'm still faster than you!"

As he was drawing in the feet of the snake and speaking so cockily, another person finished drawing his snake. That person immediately snatched the pot of wine out of his hands and said, "Have you ever seen a snake before? A snake has no legs, so why did you draw them in? A snake with legs isn't a snake, so the first person to draw a snake would be me, not you."

When finished speaking, the person tilted his head back and, as if it were a matter of course, chug-a-lugged the wine down.

The person who added feet to the snake could say nothing, just angrily watch someone else drink the jug of wine.

"Draw a snake and add feet to it" is used to describe someone who, thinking himself to be clever, does something unnecessary or creates complications, thereby outwitting himself and messing up a matter.

画 龙 点 睛

huà   lóng   diǎn   jīng

(画, draw; 龙, dragon; 点, put in; 睛, pupil)

BRING A PICTURE OF A DRAGON TO LIFE
BY PUTTING IN THE PUPILS OF ITS EYES

南北朝时期的梁朝时，有位很出名的大画家名叫张僧繇，他的绘画技术很高超。当时的皇帝梁武帝信奉佛教，修建了很多寺庙，都让张僧繇去作画。

传说，有一年梁武帝要张僧繇为金陵（现在的江苏省南京市）的安东寺作画，在寺庙的墙壁上画四条龙。他答应下来，仅用三天时间就画成了。这些龙画得栩栩如生，惟妙惟肖，简直就像真龙一样活灵活现。

张僧繇画成后，吸引很多人前来观看，都称赞画得好，太逼真了。可是，当人们走近点一看，就会发现美中不足的是四条龙全都没有眼睛。大家纷纷请求他，把龙的眼睛点上。张僧繇解释说：

"给龙点眼珠并不难，但点上了眼珠这些龙会破壁飞走的。"

大家听后谁都不相信，认为他这样解释很荒唐，墙上的龙怎么会飞走呢？日子长了，很多人都以为他是在说谎。

张僧繇被逼得没有办法，不得不答应给龙"点睛"。这一天，在寺庙墙壁前有许多人围观，张僧繇当着众人的面，提起画笔，轻轻地给两条画龙点上眼睛。奇怪的事情果然发生了，他刚点过第二条龙的眼睛，突然间天空乌云密布，狂风四起，雷鸣电闪，在雷电之中，人们亲眼看见被"点睛"的两条龙震破墙壁凌空而起，张牙舞爪地腾云驾雾飞向天空。

过一会儿，云散天晴，人们被吓得目瞪口呆，一句话也说不出来了。再看看墙壁上，只剩下了没有被点上眼睛的两条龙，而另外被"点睛"的两条龙已经不知去向了。

后来人们根据这个传说故事引申出"画龙点睛"这句成语，比喻说话或写文章，在主要处用上关键性的、精辟的一两句话，点明要旨，使内容更加生动有力。

During the Liang Dynasty of the Northern and Southern Dynasties there was a painter of remarkable skill named Zhang Sengyao. The emperor at that time, Liang Wudi, was a believer in Buddhism. He had many temples constructed, and had them all painted by Zhang Sengyao.

The story goes that one year Liang Wudi wanted Zhang Sengyao to do a wall painting of four dragons for the Andong Temple in Jinling (present day Nanjing). Zhang Sengyao accepted and completed the paintings in only three days. The dragons were vividly lifelike, as though they were actual dragons.

When Zhang Sengyao was finished, many visitors came in praise of the paintings. However, when people looked closely, they discovered that the otherwise complete dragons were all missing the pupils of their eyes. Everyone repeatedly asked that Zhang Sengyao paint in the pupils, to which he replied, "To give the dragons pupils would not be difficult, but if I did so, these dragons would break out of the wall and fly away."

Of course, no one believed this and considered this explanation to be utterly ridiculous. How could paintings of dragons fly away? As the days went by, many people felt that he was simply lying.

Zhang Sengyao was left with no recourse, and agreed to paint in the dragons' eyes. That day, many people gathered in front of the painted wall. Zhang Sengyao stood in front of the crowd and raised his brush. Deftly, he painted in the eyes of two dragons, and a strange thing occurred. Just as he finished the eyes of the second dragon, the sky suddenly was covered with thick, black clouds, a violent wind kicked up from all directions, thunder roared, and lightning flashed. In the flash of a lightning bolt, people could see that the two dragons were shaking the wall apart and rising into the air. Displaying teeth and brandishing claws, they mounted the clouds and mist and rose towards the heavens.

After a moment had passed, the skies cleared and people stood dumbfounded and speechless. Looking at the wall, only the two dragons which were not given eyes remained.

The idiom "bring a picture of a dragon to life by putting in the pupils of its eyes" is used as a metaphor for, in speech or in writing, to use a key or penetrating phrase to drive home a point and thus give the content more power.

挥 汗 成 雨

huī   hàn   chéng   yǔ ·

(挥, drip; 汗, sweat; 成, like; 雨, rain)

SWEAT DRIPS LIKE RAIN

春秋时期，齐国有位著名政治家、外交家名叫晏婴，有一年，他代表齐国去楚国访问。当时，楚国比较强大，看不起齐国，又听说来访使者晏婴是个身材短小的矮子，就想趁机当面侮辱他。

楚国事先在城门旁，特意按晏婴的身高开了个小门。打算当他来到楚国时，就让他钻小门进城。晏婴来到了楚国，到城门口一看，他明白了：这是想侮辱我。那好，看我怎么对付你们吧。便说："到狗国去才从狗门进去，难道，今天我是到狗国来了吗？"

接待的楚国官员弄巧成拙了，反倒让晏婴骂了，只好让他走大门正式进城。

晏婴到王宫拜会楚王，楚王以轻蔑的眼光，上下打量着他，说道：

"齐国没有人吗？怎么派你当国家代表？"

晏婴心想：你还要侮辱齐国和我个人，便理直气壮地说：

"齐国的都城有几百条街道，如果人们都张开袖子，就会把太阳遮蔽了：人们挥洒的汗水就像下了雨，街上的行人肩擦肩、脚碰脚，你怎么说齐国没有人呢？至于派我到贵国来嘛，那是因为我们齐国办外交有个规矩，贤明的使臣就派到贤明的国君那里，愚蠢无能的使臣就派到愚蠢无能的国君那里。我晏婴在齐国是最愚蠢无能的人，只好派到楚国来了。"

晏婴把楚王驳得张口结舌，一句话也说不上来。

后来人们根据这个故事引申出"挥汗成雨"这句成语，比喻人很拥挤，也用来形容出汗很多。

In the Spring and Autumn Period, the State of Qi had a famous statesman and diplomat named Yan Ying. One year, he was sent on an official visit to the State of Chu. At that time, Chu was a relatively powerful country, and looked with scorn upon Qi. They had also heard that this official Yan Ying was short of stature and thus sought for ways to ridicule him.

First, the Chu constructed a small door the height of Yan Ying next to the great city gate, intending to make Yan Ying use it to enter the city when he arrived. Arriving at the city gate and seeing what had been prepared, Yan Ying immediately understood that this was a plan to embarrass him. "Very well," he thought, "I shall have to counter you."

"Upon arriving in a country of dogs, one must enter through a dog door. Today, have I indeed come to such a country?"

Bested by their own attempts at cleverness, the Chu officials were mocked by Yan Ying and were forced to let him make a formal entrance using the main gate.

When Yan Ying went to call on the king of Chu, the king contemptuously looked him up and down, and said, "Does the State of Qi so lack people? How is it that you have been sent as a representative of Qi?"

Yan Ying thought, "You still want to embarrass me and my nation." Confidently, he spoke:

"The capital of the State of Qi has several hundred streets. Were its people to extend their sleeves, it would block out the sun. The sweat dripping off peoples' bodies is like a rain. On the streets people rub shoulders and step on each others' feet. How can you say that Qi lacks people? As for sending me to visit your country, we in Qi have a rule: the virtuous and able ambassadors are sent to where virtuous and able rulers are, and foolish and untalented ambassadors are sent to where foolish and untalented rulers are. Myself, I am known in Qi as a foolish and untalented person, and therefore was best dispatched to come to Chu.

Thus Yan Ying turned the king's words back on himself, leaving him flustered and tongue-tied.

The idiom "sweat drips like rain" is drawn from this story to describe a great number of people or a huge crowd. It can also be used to describe sweating a lot.

讳 疾 忌 医

huì　　jí　　jì　　yī

（讳，hide；疾，sickness；忌，be afraid；医，treatment）

HIDE ONE'S SICKNESS
FOR FEAR OF TREATMENT

中国古代有位著名的医生名叫扁鹊，他是战国时期的人，原名叫秦越人。他能医治各种疾病，常年在各地行医，医疗经验很丰富。由于他的医术很高明，又能热心为大家治病，所以，人们都把他比作传说中的神医扁鹊，称他为扁鹊大夫。

有一次，扁鹊去见蔡桓侯，他在旁边闲坐一会儿，便对蔡桓侯说："大王，您现在已经患病了，但病还在皮肤浅层的地方，只要赶快医治还来得及。不然，病情就要加重了。"

蔡桓侯微笑着说：

"我哪有什么病哟！"

扁鹊听后转身就出去了。

蔡桓侯不高兴的对左右大臣们说：

"这些医生总是医治没有患病的人，来显示自己的医术高明。"

几天后，扁鹊又见到了蔡桓侯，他惊恐地劝告说：

"大王，您的病已经发展到肌肉血脉里去了，如再不医治，病情会更加厉害的。"

蔡桓侯还是不相信自己有病，这次他是越发生气了。

十多天后，扁鹊再次见到蔡桓侯，便严重警告说：

"您的病已经侵入到内脏去了，如再不医治，就十分危险啦。"

蔡桓侯听了很是生气，根本不理睬扁鹊了。

又过了几天，扁鹊又去见蔡桓侯，对他望了望，扭头就往回走。蔡桓侯感到奇怪，就派人去问扁鹊，是什么缘故。

扁鹊对来人说：

"你们的大王不听医生的话，现在性命很危险啦！"

来人很是吃惊赶忙追问，扁鹊说：

"开始病在皮肤上，敷敷药就能好的。病发展到肌肉、内脏里，用针灸或用汤药医治，费点事还能治好。可是，现在你们大王的病已经深入到骨髓里去了，再没有什么好办法治疗了。"

几天后，蔡桓侯突然感到全身疼痛，急忙派人请扁鹊大夫，可是，此时扁鹊已经到秦国去了。没有几天，蔡桓侯因重病死去了。

后来人们根据这个故事引申出"讳疾忌医"这句成语，形容那些隐瞒或掩饰自己的缺点错误，又不想改正的人。

In ancient times there was a famous Chinese physician named Bian Que. Living during the Warring States Period, his original name was Qin Yueren. Capable of treating every kind of illness, he would travel year round offering his services. Because of his exceptional medical skill and passion for healing people, he became transformed through stories into a mythical physician known as Dr. Bian Que.

Once, Bian Que went to see Cai Huanhou. As he sat to the side resting, he said to Cai Huanhou, "O Great King, you are already beginning to suffer from disease, but the disease is only as deep as your skin. If you begin treatment now, there is still hope. If not, the disease will only get worse."

Cai Huanhou smiled and said, "Don't be ridiculous. I have no such illness."

Bian Que heard this, turned around, and left.

A bit unhappily, Cai Huanhou said to his surrounding ministers, "These doctors are always curing people that aren't sick, trying to show off their great skill."

Several days later, Bian Que again visited Cai Huanhou and advised him, alarmed, "O Great King, the disease has already progressed to the muscles and blood vessels. If no treatment is given, your condition will only get worse."

Cai Huanhou still didn't believe he was sick, and became even angrier.

Ten days later, Bian Que saw Cai Huanhou again and gravely told him, "The disease has invaded your internal organs. If no treatment is administered, the danger will be quite great."

Hearing this, Cai Huanhou grew very angry and just ignored Bian Que.

Another few days went past, and Bian Que went to see Cai Huanhou once more. He looked at him, shook his head, and went away. Cai Huanhou felt this strange, and sent someone to ask Bian Que the reason for his behavior.

Bian Que said to the servant, "Your king will not listen to the words of a doctor and thus his life is in grave danger!"

Shocked, the servant hastily made more inquiries, to which Bian Que replied, "At first, the disease was only at the skin, and an ointment would have been sufficient. When the disease progressed to the muscles and internal organs, acupuncture or a medical broth would have cured it. But now your king's illness has penetrated into his bones and there is nothing to be done."

Several days later, Cai Huanhou's whole body was suddenly wracked with pain and Bian Que was hastily sent for. However, by this time Bian Que had already moved on to the State of Qin. After a few days, Cai Huanhou was dead.

The idiom "hide one's sickness for fear of treatment" is used as a metaphor for hiding or covering up one's weak points or errors, or a person who doesn't want to amend their errors.

火 中 取 栗

huǒ　zhōng　qǔ　lì

（火，fire；中，middle；取，take；栗，chestnut）

PULL SOMEONE ELSE'S CHESTNUTS
OUT OF THE FIRE

有一只狡猾的猴子，到处寻找吃的东西。忽然，它闻到了一股香味，马上跳过去，发现一处火堆里有栗子。这是多么好吃的美餐啊！

猴子想把栗子取出来，又怕爪子被火烧伤，它急得直挠腮。正在这时候，一只花猫从这里路过，猴子见到花猫，眼睛一转，主意就有了。

"喂，花猫，我听说你的胆子小，很不勇敢，连大老鼠都不敢抓……"

还没等猴子说完，花猫很生气地说：

"这是胡说，我昨天还抓着一只大老鼠呢。"

"啊！是这样，可是我可没有看见。"

"不信，我给你表演表演。"花猫有些激动地说。

猴子趁机马上说：

"那好啊，现在就有机会表演。你看见了吗，这火堆中有烤熟的栗子，闻到香味了吧。你把它取出来，不但表现了你是勇敢的，而且还能吃到香甜可口的栗子。"

经猴子花言巧语地一说，花猫馋得直流口水，最后它同意了。

花猫把爪子伸进火堆中取出第一个栗子，栗子是取出来了，可是爪子上的毛被烧掉一些。花猫想，爪子上的毛被烧掉些，可是，过一会可以吃到栗子，所以，花猫继续一个个地取栗子。狡猾的猴子见花猫取出一个，它吃掉一个。花猫把栗子全部取出时，猴子也全都吃完了。

结果，花猫一个栗子也没有吃到，反而把爪子上的毛烧掉不少，还痛得直叫唤。这时，狡猾的猴子已经溜走了。

后来人们根据这个故事引申出"火中取栗"这句成语，用来比喻被别人欺骗、利用，干冒险的事，最后自己得不到一点好处。

Once there was a crafty monkey who was always looking for things to eat. Suddenly, he caught a whiff of something good-smelling. Running over, he discovered a pile of chestnuts in a fire. What a tasty treat!

The monkey wanted to get to the chestnuts, but was also afraid of burning his paws in the flames. He thought furiously. Just at this time, a calico cat happened to stroll by. In the wink of an eye, the monkey had an idea.

"Hey, cat, I hear you're gutless, a real chicken, and that you don't even dare to catch mice...."

Before the monkey could finish talking, the cat angrily said, "Nonsense! Why, just yesterday I caught a mouse!"

"Oh ho! But I didn't see it!"

"If you don't believe me, I'll prove it to you!" the cat said, agitated.

Seeing his opportunity, the monkey said, "Alright, there just happens to be a way to prove it right now. Look, there's some roasted chestnuts in that fire over there. Can you smell them? If you can get them out of the fire, you'll not only prove your courage, you'll also be able to eat some tasty chestnuts."

With the monkey's fine words, the cat's mouth was watering in anticipation, and it eventually agreed.

Using a paw to reach into the fire, the cat got the first chestnut out, but some of the fur was burned off. The cat thought, "The fur on my paw has been singed a bit, but in a moment I'll get to eat these chestnuts." Therefore, the calico continued to pull out the chestnuts one by one. When the cat removed a chestnut, the devilish monkey would gobble it up. When the cat had finally pulled all the chestnuts out, the monkey had eaten them all.

In the end, the calico cat didn't eat a single chestnut and his paws got badly burned besides. By this time, the monkey was already far away.

The idiom "pull someone else's chestnuts out of the fire" means to be deceived or used by someone else in doing something dangerous, with no benefit to oneself.

涸 辙 之 鲋

hé　　zhé　　zhī　　fù

（涸，dry; 辙，rut; 之，of; 鲋，a kind of fish）

A FISH STRANDED IN A DRY RUT

战国时期，有位著名的学者名叫庄周，人们尊称他为庄子。当时庄子家里很穷，生活很困难，家中经常缺粮，无米下锅。有一次，家里又没粮了，他到一个当官的家里去借。这个当官的人很吝啬，但又爱说漂亮话。他装出很大度的样子说：

"行呵，不过，得等我收了老百姓的税租之后，就借给你三百两银子，你看好吧。"

庄子听了这话很生气，心想我就是现在缺粮，若等你借我钱买粮，我可能已经饿死了。

于是，他就给这个当官的讲了一段寓言故事：

"昨天，我到你这儿来的时候，在半路上忽然听到叫喊救命的声音，我低头一看，原来是大路中间干涸的车辙中躺着一条鲋鱼。我便问它：

'鲋鱼啊，你怎么到这儿来了呢？'

鲋鱼说：

'我是从东海里来的，不幸落到这车辙里。车辙里的水快要被太阳晒干了，我也快干死了。请你给我一些水救救我吧！'

我连忙点头答应，说：

'行啊，我现在就动身去南方，看望吴、越两国国君。那里的水很多，我说服他们，把西江的水引到这里来。小鱼，你看好吧！'

鲋鱼听了我的话，很气愤地说：

'你竟说大话，我失去了水，在这车辙里就活不成了。我只需要一点水就能活命，等到你把西江水引到这里，我早就死了，到那时，你去干鱼店找我吧。'"

当官的听了庄子讲的寓言，什么话也说不出来了。

以后人们根据庄子的寓言故事引申出"涸辙之鲋"这句成语，比喻处境十分困难，迫切需要救援和帮助。

During the Warring States Period there was a famous thinker named Zhuang Zhou, also known honorifically as Zhuang Zi. At that time Zhuang Zi lived a difficult life. He was very poor and often lacked grain or rice for his pot. One time he ran out of grain again and went to borrow some from an official. This official was very miserly but liked to speak sweetly. Putting on big airs, he said, "No problem, but you'll have to wait until I collect taxes and rents from the populace. Then I'll lend you three hundred taels of silver, alright?"

At these words, Zhuang Zi became angry, thinking that if he had to wait before he could get some grain, he could well starve to death.

Thus, he told the official a little parable:

"Yesterday, when I was on my way here, I suddenly heard a little voice crying for help from the road. Looking down, I saw a carp lying in the rut of a wagon wheel. I asked him, `Hey carp, what are you doing here?'

"The carp answered, 'I come from the East Ocean and have had the misfortune to land in this wheel rut. The water in here has been almost all dried up by the sun, and I will soon die. Please give me half a cup of water to save my life!'

"Hurriedly I nodded my head and promised I would do so, saying, 'Alright. I'll set off for the south and go visit the kings of Wu and Yue. There's a lot of water there, and I'll convince them to divert the Xi River up here. How about that little fish!'

"The carp listened to me and then said furiously, 'You dare speak such big words. I'm losing water and dying in a wheel rut. All I need is a cup of water to save my life. If you go to bring the Xi River here, I will be long dead, and you'll be able to find me in the dried fish market.' "

When the official heard this parable of Zhuang Zi's, he had

nothing to say.

The idiom "a fish stranded in a dry rut" is used as a metaphor for being stuck in difficult circumstances and in need of urgent help.

江 郎 才 尽

jiāng láng cái jìn

（江, a surname; 郎, young man; 才, talent; 尽, exhaust）

A JIANGLANG DEPLETED OF HIS TALENTS

南北朝时期，有个人名叫江淹，在幼年时，父亲就死去了。他的家境很贫穷，常常挖野菜当饭吃。到了 13 岁时，他便上山打柴，卖几个钱，养活母亲。

尽管环境很艰苦，江淹仍然刻苦读书，好学不倦。后来他的诗文都写的很好，深受大家的赞赏和敬慕，人们称他为"江郎"。当时朝廷也很器重他，皇上封他当了大官。

江郎在年轻时很有才气。可是，后来他却写不出什么好文章了，并且越来越退步。人们都说他"才气已尽"了。这是什么原因造成的呢？这里有些传说：

有一次，江郎乘船，夜里船停在河边，他在船舱里睡觉，梦见一个自称名为张景阳的人来找他说：

"我以前曾借给你一匹绵缎（古代有时当纸用），现在你应当还给我了。"

江郎便把身边剩下的几尺锦缎还给他了。从此以后，江郎写的文章越来越不好了。

又有一次，江郎在家里睡觉，梦见一个自称是郭璞的人，对他说：

"我那只五色笔，放在你这儿好多年了，现在该还给我了。"

江郎从怀中取出那只五色笔还给他了。从此后，他再也写不出那些美丽的诗句了。

其实，这些传说并不是江郎晚年写不出诗文的真正原因。

真实的原因是江郎出名以后已经满足做了官，并且官越做越大，在优裕的生活中，他不再上进了；还由于他当官后高高在上，脱离群众、脱离生活。所以，写不出什么好作品，并且越来越写不好，逐年退步，才气已尽了。

后来人们根据江郎的事引申出"江郎才尽"这句成语，比喻很有学问的人，或是很有才华的作家，如果不继续努力上进，思想会僵化，才气会减退。

During the Northern and Southern Dynasties there was a man named Jiang Yan, whose father passed away when he was very young. His family was incredibly poor and often had to go digging for wild vegetables in order to eat. By age 13 he would go to the mountains to chop firewood to sell for some spare change to support his mother.

Although life was hard, Jiang Yan still worked hard at his studies, never tiring of learning. He became good at writing poetry, which won the praise and admiration of everyone. People began calling him "Jianglang" (Young Jiang). He was also regarded highly by the imperial court, and was made an official by edict of the emperor.

Jianglang was full of talent when young, but later didn't produce any writing of value. People said that his talent was all used up. A legend tells the reasons for this:

One time, Jianglang was on a boat that stopped on a riverbank for the night. Asleep in his cabin, he dreamed that a person calling himself Zhang Jingyang came looking for him, saying, "In the past I lent you a bolt of brocade for writing, and now you should return it to me."

Jianglang then gave the remainder of the brocade to him, after which his writing began to decline.

Another time Jianglang was asleep at home, when he dreamed of a man calling himself Guo Pu, who said to him, "I have left my pen here for many years, but now you must return it to me."

Jianglang removed the pen from his breast pocket and returned it. Afterwards, he never wrote another beautiful poem.

In fact, these legends don't give the real reasons why Jianglang's writings deteriorated in his later years.

The real reason was that after Jianglang became an official, he began living in comfort. Self-satisfied, he progressed no further. Moreover, he became separated from people, life, and reality. As a result, he didn't produce any more great works, and in fact his writing began to deteriorate and his talent dried up.

The story of Jianglang later gave rise to the idiom "a Jianglang depleted of his talents," which is used to describe a person of great learning or talent, who, through failure to persist in improving himself, develops an obsolete way of thinking or loses their talent.

金玉其外　败絮其中

jīn　yù　qí　wài　　bài　xù　qí　zhōng

（金，gold；玉，jade；其，its；外，outside；
败，wither；絮，cotton fiber；其，its；中，middle）

OLD COTTON FIBER COATED
IN GOLD AND JADE

从前，在杭州城里有一个卖水果的小贩，做水果生意已经好多年了。他很会贮藏柑橘一类的鲜果，不论经过冬天，还是夏天，他保存的柑橘，就如同刚从树上摘下来一样金黄，非常新鲜。尽管他卖的柑橘价格抬高了很多，但仍然有很多人买。

一天，有一个人花了大价钱，从他那里买了几个柑橘。回家切开一看，发现里边的果肉早已枯得像一团旧棉絮一样了。再切开其他几个柑橘，全都是这样，根本不能吃。所以，这个人很生气，便去找小贩，质问：

"你的柑橘皮色新鲜而内里却干枯得像棉絮，是骗人的。这样做生意太不应该了。"

小贩笑笑，满不在乎地回答：

"我做水果生意已经好多年了，我愿意卖，人家愿意买，从没有人责问我，怎么就你不满意呢？"

小贩越说越激动，又说：

"什么叫应该、不应该？难道世上耍欺编手段的，就我一个人吗？那些身居高职的文武官员们骑大马、坐大轿、吃的好、穿的好，一个个好像是国家的栋梁，真有治理国家的本领吗？其实，哪一个不是装得一本正经。这些人都是徒有虚表，哪个不像我的柑橘一样'金玉其外，败絮其中'呢？你为什么看不到这帮人，只看到我的柑橘呢？为什么你不去责问他们，反倒来责问我这个卖水果的小贩呢？"

这个小贩借这个机会，把当时的封建官吏痛骂了一顿。

买柑橘的人听后，也不再说话了。

后来人们从这个故事中引申出"金玉其外"这个成语，比喻只有华丽的外表，而没有实际本领的人；除了形容人，还可比喻外表好看，里面一团糟的事。

Once there was a fruit peddler in the city of Hangzhou who had sold fruit for many, many years. He was very capable at keeping citrus fruits so that whether in winter or summer, his oranges and tangerines were as fresh and golden yellow as if they had just been plucked off the tree. Although the prices for these fruits were very high, many people still bought them.

One day, a man spent a great deal of money to buy several pounds of oranges from this fruit seller. After returning home and cutting one open, he discovered that the flesh was as dried and withered as a wad of old cotton fiber. All of the oranges turned out the same, and thus, inedible. Angrily, the man sought out the peddler, questioning him thus:

"Your oranges look nice and fresh from on the outside but the insides are as shriveled as cotton! This is thievery, not a proper way to run a business!"

The fruit seller laughed, and answered offhandedly, "I've been selling fruit for years now; what I sell, people buy. No one has ever thought to take me task before, so why do you dissatisfied?"

As the fruit seller spoke, he became more and more excited, "What do you mean by `proper' anyway? Am I the only one on earth who cheats people? Those high and mighty officials, up on their high horses, riding in their big sedan chairs, eating well, wearing fancy clothes — each of them acts like he is the pillar of the state, but do any of them have the talent to manage a nation? In fact, there's not a one that doesn't pretend to be decent, but there's not a one that really deserves to be called so. Which one isn't like my oranges: fair without and foul within? Why do you ignore that gang, but have eyes for my oranges? How come you don't call them to account, but take to task a fruit peddler?"

The fruit peddler took advantage of this situation to round-ly curse the feudal officials of the time.

The man who had bought the fruits didn't utter another peep.

The idiom "old cotton fiber coated in gold and jade" came to be used to describe one who, with fine appearance, does not have any real ability.

惊 弓 之 鸟

jīng   gōng   zhī   niǎo

(惊, start; 弓, bow; 之, of; 鸟, bird)

A BIRD THAT STARTS AT
THE TWANG OF A BOWSTRING

古时候，魏国有一个很有名望的射箭能手叫更羸，他的射箭技巧很高超，能做到百发百中。

有一天，天空格外清朗，魏王带着更羸等人到郊外去打猎。当他们来到郊外，向天空望去，过了一会儿，从东边飞过来一只大雁，它慢慢地飞着，边飞边鸣叫。这时候，更羸手指天空飞着的这只大雁，对魏王说：

"大王，您看见这只大雁了吧。"

魏王说："嗯，看见了。"

更羸信心十足地说：

"我不用箭，只要拉一下弓，扣一下弦，就能把这只大雁射下来。"

"是真的吗？"魏王不相信自己的耳朵，用怀疑的口气问道：

"你有这样的本事？"

更羸又说："那就让我试一试吧。"

更羸并没有取箭，只见他左手托弓，右手拉弦，只听得 "嘣"的一声响。同时，只见那只大雁直往上飞，拍打两下翅膀，忽然就从半空中直掉下来了。

"啊！"魏王直瞪着眼睛看着，大吃一惊地说：

"你真有这样的本事呀！"

这时，更羸微笑地解释说：

"并不是我的本事大，也没有什么稀奇的，是因为我知道这是一只受过伤、又失群的大雁。"

魏王更加奇怪了，便问道：

"你是怎么知道的呢？"

更羸进一步解释说：

"您看它飞得很慢，那么倦乏，鸣叫声也很凄惨。飞得慢，这是因为它受过了箭伤，伤口没有愈合，还很疼痛；叫得凄惨，是因为它离开同伴，孤单失群得不到大家的帮助。所以，它一听到弦响，心里很害怕，就拼命往高处飞，这样一使劲，伤口又裂开了，它就掉下来了。"

后来人们根据这个故事引申出"惊弓之鸟"这句成语，来比喻受过惊吓或打击之后，再遇到类似的情况就惊慌害怕。

In ancient times, in the State of Wei lived a well-known archer named Geng Lei. His skill with the bow was exceptional, and could hit the bull's-eye a hundred times out of a hundred.

One exceptionally clear day, the king of Wei took Geng Lei and others to the countryside to go hunting. Once in the countryside, they all began searching the skies for game. After a moment, a lone wild goose came flying slowly from the east, calling as it flew. Geng Lei pointed to the goose and said to the king, "Does Your Majesty see that goose?"

The king replied, "Yes, I see it."

Geng Lei confidently said, "Without using an arrow, I can simply pluck my bowstring and shoot that goose down."

"Really?" The king couldn't believe his own ears, and skeptically asked, "Do you have such a skill?"

Geng Lei said, "Please allow me to try."

Without drawing an arrow, Geng Lei took up his bow in his left hand and drew back the string with his right. There was a loud "twang!" Simultaneously, everyone saw the goose climb straight up, furiously beating its wings. Suddenly, it dropped from the sky.

"Wow!" exclaimed the king, looking up. Amazed, he said, "You <u>do</u> have such skill!"

Geng Lei smiled and explained, "It's not really my skill, nor is it anything mysterious. It's because I knew that this goose had been injured before, and had also lost its flock."

The king was even more puzzled, and asked, "How could you know such things?"

Geng Lei explained further, "Your Majesty saw how slow and wearily the goose was flying, and how wretched its call was. It was flying so slowly because it had been shot by an arrow before, and the wound had not yet totally healed, and it hurt. It was calling so pitifully because it had lost its flock and had lost the help of others. Therefore, when it heard the twang of the bow, it felt fear and began to climb higher with all its life. Because of such exertion, the wound opened again, and down it came."

The idiom "a bird that starts at the twang of a bowstring" came to be used to describe one who, having been frightened or attacked in the past, is stricken with fear in a similar situation later.

精 卫 填 海

jīng　　wèi　　tián　　hǎi

（精卫, a kind of bird; 填, fill; 海, sea）

THE BIRD JINGWEI TRYS TO
FILL UP THE SEA WITH PEBBLES

传说，在很久很久以前的上古时代，炎帝神农氏有个小女儿名叫女娃，她活泼可爱。

女娃经常到东海去游玩。有一天，她又到东海边游玩，在柔软的沙滩上，玩耍着美丽的贝壳。玩的高兴，女娃便下海游泳。突然间，海面刮起了狂风，波涛汹涌，不幸她被卷到海里淹死了。

女娃死后变成一只小鸟。这只小鸟美丽勇敢，它的头上有不同颜色的花纹，嘴如一块白玉，身披乌黑发亮的羽衣，一双红脚支撑着身体。它在东海上面飞来飞去，不停地呼唤着"精卫、精卫，"因此，人们就叫它"精卫"鸟。

女娃感叹自己年纪轻轻就被无情的大海吞没了，她也担心别人再被东海淹死，所以，她发誓要把东海填平。

精卫鸟每天飞到西山，衔着这里的小树枝、小石头，飞到东海上空，再投入大海，每天往返多次。

宽大的东海嘲笑精卫说：

"小鸟儿，你算了吧，你用小树枝和小石头，何时能把我填平呢？你就是花费一万年，也别想把我填平，我可是大海呀！"

精卫鸟坚定地回答：

"不！就是一万年，一百万年，我也要把你填平的。"

从此，精卫鸟更加努力，坚持不懈地，不断衔着树枝、石头投入大海，天天如此，年年如此，决心要把东海填平。

以后人们根据这个神话故事引申出"精卫填海"这句成语，比喻只要按既定的目标，以顽强的精神，坚韧不拔地奋斗到底，无论做什么事情都一定会取得成功的。

In ancient times, in the remotest reaches of time, there was a lovely and spirited young woman named Nu Wa who came from the clan of the legendary ruler Yan Di.

Nu Wa often came to the East China Sea to play. One day she came and was playing with pretty seashells on the soft-sanded beach. Carefree, she dove under the water for a swim. Instantly, a fierce wind kicked up and waves began surging turbulently. Nu Wa was caught up in the waves and drowned.

After death, Nu Wa turned into a beautiful and brave little bird. Its head was covered with many colors and its beak was like a piece of white jade. Its body was draped in shining black feathers, and a pair of red feet supported it. It flew back and forth over the East China Sea, crying out, "jingwei, jingwei." Therefore, people called it the Jingwei bird.

Nu Wa sighed over being swallowed up by the unfeeling ocean when she was still young, and was worried that others might meet the same fate. Thus, she swore that she would fill in the East China Sea.

Several times each day the Jingwei would fly to the West Mountains, pick up a twig or pebble and go drop it the East China Sea.

The broad and vast East China Sea laughed scornfully at the Jingwei, "Little bird, think a moment! How long will it take you to fill me in using little twigs and pebbles? Not in ten thousand years could you fill me in, for I am the Great Ocean!"

The Jingwei answered determinedly, "No! I will fill you in if it takes ten thousand years or a million years!"

Thereafter, the Jingwei worked even harder, continuing to throw twigs and stones in the ocean. Day after day, year after year, she doggedly sought to fill in the East China Sea.

This story gave rise to the idiom "the bird Jingwei trys to fill up the sea with pebbles," which means to indomitably persist in carrying out a set objective or sticking with something to the very end to obtain success no matter what.

橘 化 为 枳

jú huà wéi zhì

（橘, orange；化为, become；
枳, a kind of fruit apparently like orange）

AN ORANGE BECOMES ANOTHER VARIETY
WHEN TRANSPLANTED

春秋时期，齐国有位著名的政治家、外交家名叫晏婴，人很机智，会讲话、会办事，能摆事实讲道理。他在各国都很出名，大家都很尊敬他，称他为晏子。

有一次，齐王派他到楚国去商谈国事。楚国国王也知道晏子很有名气，但也想亲自了解一下晏子到底有多大的本领。

晏子到楚国后，楚王设酒宴亲自招待他。正在二人喝酒谈话时，两个军士押着一个犯人，从大厅门口走过，一边走着，一边大声喝斥着。楚王故意惊奇地问：

"我在宴请客人，你们吵嚷什么？"

"两个军士赶忙上前禀告说："报告大王，我们抓到一个盗窃犯。"

"他是哪里人，竟敢在大白天偷抢东西。"楚王站起来发问。

军士又说："他是齐国人。"

楚王看看晏子，想看他有什么反应，而晏子继续在喝酒，表现出丝毫不在意的样子。

楚王就把话挑明了，嘲弄地对晏子说：

"哦，是齐国人，你们齐国人都习惯偷窃东西吧？"

晏子听了这话，马上站起来说：

"大王，您这些话说的没有道理吧。我听说柑橘树生长在淮南就能结出甜美的柑橘，如果将它移栽到淮北，就生出苦涩难吃的枳子。尽管它们的叶子很相似，但味道却不同。这是什么原因呢？这就是因为水土不同造成的。这个人生活在我们齐国，从不偷窃，可是到了你们楚国，却变成盗贼了。这恐怕是因为你们楚国的风俗习惯使他变坏了的吧。"

晏子这一席话，说的楚王直瞪眼睛，好半天没有说出话。

人们根据这个故事引申出"橘化为枳"这句成语。比喻由于环境的影响，而使人变好或变坏。

During the Spring and Autumn Period, there was a famous statesman and diplomat from the State of Qi named Yan Ying, who was resourceful, well-spoken, competent, and reasonable. Having made a name for himself in each state, he gained people's respect, who called him Yan Zi.

One time, the king of Qi dispatched Yan Zi to the State of Chu to hold official negotiations. The king of Chu had heard of Yan Zi's fame, but wanted to see for himself how talented he actually was.

After Yan Zi arrived in Chu, the king of Chu personally received him in a banquet. As the two were drinking and talking, two soldiers entered, escorting a prisoner, and noisily approached the king. Pretending to be astonished, the king asked, "I'm entertaining a guest! What are you making a racket about?"

The two soldiers quickly came forward and reported, "We are informing Your Majesty that we have captured a thief."

"Where is he from, that he would dare steal in broad daylight?" the king asked, standing up.

A soldier answered, "He is from the State of Qi."

The king looked at Yan Zi for a reaction, but Yan Zi continued to drink his wine, as if not paying the slightest attention.

Unable to keep his words back, the king mockingly said to Yan Zi, "Hmph. A man of Qi. Are all people from Qi in the habit of thievery?"

Yan Zi heard these words and then abruptly stood.

"Your Majesty's words are unreasonable. I hear that an orange tree grown to the south of the River Huai produces sweet and fair fruit. But if it is transplanted to the north of the river, its fruit becomes bitter and inedible. Although their leaves may be similar, the two tastes are very different. What is the reason for this? It is a result of differences in the soil and water. Now, this man once lived in the State of Qi, where he never stole anything.

But now he has come to Chu and has become a thief. I'm afraid that this is because he has been stained by the customs and habits of the people of your country."

Yan Zi's speech struck the king silent, and he remained speechless for a long time.

The idiom "an orange becomes another variety when transplanted" is used to describe the effects of the environment on people's behavior.

克 己 奉 公

kè　jǐ　fèng　gōng

(克, be strict with; 己, oneself; 奉, devote to; 公, public interest)

BE WHOLEHEARTEDLY DEVOTED
TO PUBLIC DUTY

东汉时候，有个名叫祭遵的人，在光武帝手下负责军队法令工作。他很受人尊敬，虽然家里很有钱，可他的生活很俭朴，常把光武帝赏给自己的财物，都奖给他的部下，所以大家都称赞祭遵的为人。

祭遵对主管的军法工作一贯认真负责，严肃公正，从不讲私人情面。有一次，光武帝的身边随从在外边犯法了。祭遵把此人抓起来，立刻查明了真实情况，按军法把这个随从处以死刑。

光武帝知道后很生气，下令把祭遵抓了起来，一定要拿他问罪。这时一个大臣出来劝光武帝说：

"大王，可不能这么做啊！"

"为什么就不能拿祭遵问罪！"光武帝怒气冲冲地说。

大臣说："祭遵能严格要求自己，克制自己的私心，做事谨慎小心，处处以公为重，大王平时不是要求部队要严守号令吗？现在祭遵能严明执法，不讲私情是应当称赞的。这么好的人，您还要抓起来问罪，这会影响您在军队中的威信的。"

光武帝听了劝告，就把祭遵释放了，并表彰了他。

有一次，光武帝对将领们说：

"大家都知道了，连我的随从犯了法祭遵也要依法论罪，他更不会对别人讲私人情面了。"

人们根据这个故事引申出"克己奉公"这句成语。比喻克制自己私欲，一切依公办事。现在用这个成语，来称颂严格要求自己，一心为公的人。

During the Eastern Han Dynasty there was a man named Zhai Zun, appointed by Emperor Guang Wu to be in charge of military laws and decrees. He gained people's respect, for though he was from a wealthy family, he lived simply and often gave distributed gifts from the emperor to his subordinates. Thus people praised him for his conduct.

Zhai Zun was consistently steadfast and upright in his management of military law, never looking for personal advantage. One time, a member of the emperor's entourage broke the law. Zhai Zun arrested the offender, immediately held an investigation, and executed the man according to military law.

When Emperor Guang Wu heard about this, he was furious, and issued an order to arrest and denounce Zhai Zun. At this point a minister came forward and advised the emperor, "Your Highness, this cannot be done!"

"Why cannot Zhai Zun be condemned!" the emperor said in a towering fury.

The minister continued, "Zhai Zun places strict demands on himself and restrains his personal feelings. He is meticulous in his work, and placed the public interest first. Doesn't Your Highness normally require his troops to strictly obey orders? That Zhai Zun is now impartially enforcing the law with no regard for personal interest should be worthy of praise. If Your Highness arrests and condemns such a fine person, it will undermine your prestige within the army."

After listening to this advice, the emperor released Zhai Zun and issued him a commendation.

Later, Emperor Guang Wu addressed his generals, and said, "You all know that Zhai Zun dared to execute one of my entourage who had broken the law, so he certainly will not give in to personal feelings for others."

This story gave rise to the idiom "be wholeheartedly devoted to public duty." It describes a suppression of personal desires and a total commitment to the public good. Today it is used as praise for placing strict demands on oneself and serving the public.

刻 舟 求 剑

kè　　zhōu　　qiú　　jiàn

（刻，nick；舟，boat；求，seek；剑，sword）

NICK THE BOAT TO SEEK THE SWORD

古时候，楚国有一个人，在他坐船过江的时候，一不小心，把身上挂的一把宝剑掉进江里去了。

那个人不慌不忙地从衣袋里取出一把小刀，在船舷上落下宝剑的地方刻了一个记号。嘴里自言自语嘱咐自己：

"别忘记了，我的宝剑是从这儿掉下去的。"

同船人见他不着急的样子都很纳闷，就问他：

"为什么不赶快下水捞宝剑？你在船舷上刻个记号有什么用呀？"

那个人很平静地说：

"着什么急，我的宝剑是从这个地方掉下去的，等船靠岸了，我就要从这个刻有记号的地方跳下水去，把宝剑找回来。"

过一会，船到了目的地，停下来靠了码头，这个人便从船上刻的记号处，跳下水去捞宝剑，可是，摸了好长时间也没有找到。

同船的人看到他这样寻找宝剑都感到很可笑，有一个人说：

"宝剑掉进江里以后，船还是在行走的，而宝剑沉在水底下是不会跟着走的。事实上，现在船离开丢剑的地方已经很远了，再按船舷上刻记号处去找它，怎么能找到呢？"

大家都议论说："这个人连一个很普通的道理也不懂得呢。"

后来人们根据这个故事引申出刻舟求剑这句成语，比喻人们做事情要从客观实际出发，注意事物的发展变化，来处理事情。

In ancient times there was a man from the State of Chu who was crossing a river in a boat one day and through sudden carelessness, dropped his sword in the water.

Not hurrying, the man withdrew a small knife from his pocket and carved a mark just below the railing at the spot where he dropped the sword overboard. Mumbling, he told himself, "Don't forget, the sword went over at this spot."

The other passengers were puzzled at his calmness, and asked him, "Why don't you hurry up and dive in and retrieve your sword? What good will that mark you carved do?"

Unperturbed, the man replied, "What's the rush? My sword went over at this spot, so I'll just wait till we're at shore, dive in at where I made this mark, and get the sword."

After a while, the boat arrived at its destination and moored at a pier. The man then jumped in the water at the mark he made and began looking for his sword. He felt around for a long time without finding it.

The other passengers laughed at the man's attempts to find his sword, and someone said, "After your sword fell in the river, the boat kept moving, but the sword couldn't follow. In fact, the boat is now far from the place where the sword went in. How can you possibly find your sword by a mark made on the side of the boat?"

Everyone commented to each other, "This man doesn't even understand the simplest common sense."

Today the idiom "nick the boat to seek the sword" is used to teach the lesson that people must do things in accordance with reality, paying attention to developments or changes in circumstances.

空　中　楼　阁

kōng　zhōng　lóu　gé

（空中, in the air; 楼阁, castle）

CASTLES IN THE AIR

从前有个大财主，他很愚蠢，又很固执，为此常常闹出笑话。

有一天，他到邻县去拜访一个财主。见到这个财主住的是一幢新建的三层楼房，这楼房建筑得高大漂亮，宽敞明亮，很有气派。他十分羡慕。

在回家的路上，他想，论钱财，我不比他少，我为什么不也造一座这样舒适阔气的楼房呢。

回家后，他找到了建造那所楼房的木匠，问他："那幢三层楼房是你造的吗？"

"是我造的。"木匠回答说。

财主又说："那好，你也照那样子，再给我造一幢，成吗？"

木匠同意了。

不久，这个木匠组织了其他工匠开始动工了。大家掘土、打地基、备木料等，分头干起来。

这个大财主恨不得马上能建造成，他天天到工地来，东望望西看看，但越看越不称心。好多天过去了，楼房还没有建起来，大财主就生气地质问那个木匠：

"你们这么多人忙着，用这么多材料，准备干什么？"

木匠听他这么说有些惊奇，回答说：

"你不是要造三层楼房吗，造三层楼房就需要这么多人，这么多材料啊！"

大财主急忙说：

"你们搞错了，搞错了，我只要最上面那一层，不要下面两层，你们把第三层建造出来就行了。"

木匠见财主说话认真的样子，真是哭笑不得，只好耐着性子向他解释说：

"这是不可能的，不先造第一层，就不能盖第二层，没有第一、二层，怎么能建造出第三层呢？"

这个蠢财主还是坚持着：

"你们给我干活就得听我的，我只要第三层楼房。"

木匠反驳他说：

"那不成了空中楼阁了吗！这空中楼阁谁也不能建造出来的。"

后来邻近的人们都听说财主要建造空中楼阁，大家把它当成笑料传开了。

　　人们根据这个故事引申出"空中楼阁"这句成语，比喻脱离实际的，不可能实现的计划、理论或是虚构的事物。

Once upon a time there was a very wealthy man who was both stupid and stubborn, and often made a fool of himself.

One day he went to a neighboring county to call on another wealthy man. When he saw the new three-storied house this man lived in he was envious, for the architecture was extraordinarily beautiful, spacious, and bright.

On the road home, he thought to himself, "When it comes to money, I've got as much as he does. Why don't I build such a cozy place ozf my own?"

After arriving home, he sought out the carpenter who built the house and asked him, "Was it you that built that three-storied house?"

"I built it," the carpenter answered.

The wealthy man said, "Good. I want you to build me a house exactly like that one, OK?"

The carpenter agreed.

Not long after, the carpenter had got a group of workmen together to start on the project. They excavated earth, built a foundation, and prepared lumber.

The wealthy man was impatient to get his house built. He visited the site daily to look around, and grew more and more dissatisfied. After many days had gone by, the building still hadn't come up, and he angrily questioned the carpenter, "You've got all these people and all this material! What are you planning to do!"

The carpenter listened to him somewhat curiously, and answered, "Didn't you want a three-storied house? Such a large structure needs this many people, this much material!"

Flustered, the man said, "You've got it all wrong, all wrong! I just want the top floor, not the bottom two! Just build me the top floor is all!"

The carpenter saw that the man was serious and didn't know whether to laugh or cry. He just patiently explained, "That's impossible. If you don't build the first story, you can't build the second story. If you don't have the first and second stories, how can you possibly build a third?"

The foolish moneybags persisted, "If you work for me, you do things as I want them, and I only want the third story."

The carpenter refuted him, saying, "Well, neither I nor anyone else can build a castle in the air."

Later, all the neighbors heard about the wealthy man's idea and the story quickly became material for jokes and jests.

The phrase "castles in the air" has been extended to describe a plan or theory which is impractical or has no basis in reality.

滥 竽 充 数

làn　yú　chōng　shù

（滥, indiscriminate; 竽, a kind of wind instrument;
充数, make up the number）

PASS ONESELF OFF
AS ONE OF THE PLAYERS IN AN ENSEMBLE

古代有一种用竹管编成的，样子像笙的乐器叫竽，吹奏起来很好听。

战国时期，齐国的齐宣王为了寻欢作乐，在宫廷里专门设一个大乐队为他演奏。他特别喜欢听用竽吹奏的音乐，又喜欢讲排场。吹竽的乐队就有300多人，经常叫这么多人一齐吹竽给他听，而乐工的待遇也是很优厚的。

有个南郭先生，听说齐宣王爱听竽的合奏，他本来不会吹竽，但见到有很优厚的待遇便想混进乐队里。于是，他买了竽去见齐宣王，吹嘘自己会吹竽，吹得如何好。齐宣王本来就喜欢乐队的人越多越好，所以没有多问，就把他留下来编在乐队里。

每次乐队吹竽时，南郭先生就在里边，学着别人，好象会吹的样子，也鼓着腮帮捂着竽眼儿，摇头晃脑，装模作样地在乐队里充数。

南郭先生混过一次又一次，三年过去了，谁也没有发现，每次同其他乐工得到同样的优厚赏赐。

后来，齐宣王死了，他的儿子齐湣王继承了王位。

齐湣王同他父亲一样也喜欢听吹竽的演奏，但他不喜欢合奏，嫌大乐队太吵人了，而喜欢独奏。于是，他叫乐工们一个一个地吹奏。

南郭先生看到这种情况，知道不能在乐队中充数了，再混下去怕现出原形，在别人独奏时，就偷偷地溜掉了。

后来人们根据这个故事引申出"滥竽充数"这句成语，比喻没有真实本领，而混在行家中只会装样子充数的人。

In ancient times there was a kind of pleasant sounding wind instrument called the *yu*.

During the Warring States Period, the king of the State of Qi assembled in the palace a special orchestra for his pleasure. He especially loved the sound of the *yu*, and went in for extravagance as well. The *yu* orchestra had over 300 people, and were often all called to play together for the king. Moreover, the king's musicians were all treated very well.

A man named Nanguo heard how the king loved to hear ensembles of *yu*. Though he couldn't play the *yu*, when he saw how well the musicians lived, he wanted to find a way to sneak into their number. To do this he purchased a *yu* and met with the king, emptily boasting of how well he could play. The king was always happy to add more players to his orchestra, so he admitted Nanguo without much questioning.

Each time the *yu* players performed, Nanguo was among them, copying the other musicians, puffing out his cheeks, swaying his head, and pretending to play.

Three years went by and Nanguo kept up his ruse time after time without being discovered. Each time, along with the other musicians, he would receive a handsome reward.

Later, the king passed away and his son ascended the throne.

The new king, like his father, also loved to hear the *yu*. However, he thought orchestras too noisy, and preferred solo performances. Thus, he began inviting each musician to perform one at a time.

When Nanguo saw this, he knew that he wouldn't be able to get away with hiding in the crowd anymore, and quietly slipped away.

The idiom "pass oneself off as one of the players in an ensemble" has been derived from this story to describe one who has no actual skill but only goes through the motions of a certain job in order to fill out the numbers.

梁 上 君 子

liáng shàng jūn zǐ

（梁，beam；上，on；君子，gentleman）

GENTLEMAN ON THE BEAM

东汉时期，有个人名叫陈寔，他心地善良，办事公道。此外，他也很会教育自己的子女。

一天晚上，当夜深人静时，有一个小偷溜进陈寔家里，小偷先躲在房梁上，想等这家主人睡觉后，再下去偷东西；可是，当小偷刚进陈寔的屋里时，就已经被他发现了；但是，陈寔并没有马上叫喊："抓贼"，装作没有看见一样。他穿好衣服后，就把儿孙们叫醒来到自己住的房间里。陈寔严肃认真地教育他们：

"作一个人，就要严格要求自己，自觉地要求上进，任何时候都要勉励自己，不要放松自己，不然就会走到邪路上了。干坏事情的人，并不是一生下来就是坏人，而是平时对自己要求不严，不学好，慢慢染上了坏习惯，变坏了，干些损害他人利益的事，本来这些人严格要求自己也可以做君子的。"

陈寔说到这里，马上用手指向房梁上边说：

"他就是变坏了，落到这个地步，成了梁上君子了。"

梁上的小偷亲眼看见陈寔把家人都召集到这屋里，一直用眼睛盯着陈寔，并留心听他说的每句话，感到非常羞愧。当听到最后是说自己时，先是吃惊，随后就急忙地爬下来。哆哩哆嗦地趴在地上，一个劲给陈寔叩头。陈寔的儿孙们要找绳索捆绑小偷，但被他制止了。陈寔见小偷苦苦求饶，便说：

"看你这个样子，并不像是个坏人，是生活有困难，才走上邪路的吧，你以后要学好，不要当小偷了。"

说完，让家人取出两匹绢，送给小偷。

小偷痛哭流涕，感恩不尽地一再表示今后决不当小偷了，要重新做人。

人们根据这个故事引申出"梁上君子"这句成语，用来比喻脱离实际的人，或用作小偷、窃贼的别称。

During the Eastern Han Dynasty there was a kind and just man named Chen Shi who brought his children up very well.

One evening, in the still of the night, a burglar slipped into Chen Shi's house. Hiding himself in the rafters, he was waiting for everyone to go to sleep. However, as soon as the burglar entered the room, he was discovered by Chen Shi. Chen Shi did not immediately cry out, "Thief," but pretended that he hadn't seen a thing. Calling his children into his room, he began a serious lecture:

"To be a human being, one must place strict demands on oneself, consciously demanding that one always improve. One must urge oneself at all times and never relax. Otherwise, it is easy to follow a path of wickedness. Those who do evil are not born evil, they slowly turn bad for lack of personal vigilance and a failure to study good. Those who harm others for personal benefit could have become gentlemen if they only demanded enough of themselves."

At this point, Chen Shi pointed to the rafters and said, "This man has become evil and has come to this. He has become a gentleman on the beam."

The burglar had watched the old man call his family into the room. Watching him and listening intently to his every word, he was ashamed. When he heard himself being spoken of, he was at first frightened, and climbing down, lay trembling on the ground, kowtowing at Chen Shi's feet. Chen Shi's children and grandchildren wanted to find a rope and tie the thief up, but he restrained them. Chen Shi looked at the burglar begging for mercy and said, "You do not look like a bad man, but one who has had a difficult life and chosen a path of wrongdoing. You should turn over a new leaf— don't be a thief any more!"

After he finished speaking, he made his family fetch two bolts of silk brocade, which he gave to the thief.

Weeping bitterly, the thief gave gratitude and promised again and again that from that day forth he would not steal.

Today, "gentleman on the beam" is used as a euphemism for a thief or burglar.

老 马 识 途

lǎo　mǎ　shí　tú

(老, old; 马, horse; 识, know; 途, way)

AN OLD HORSE KNOWS THE WAY

春秋时期，北方的少数民族国家山戎国侵犯燕国，为此，燕国请求齐国援助。当时齐国很强大，根据盟约的规定，齐桓公亲自带兵前去援救，随军参加讨伐的还有齐国著名大臣管仲等人。

齐国军队打败了山戎国，但是，山戎国国王逃往孤竹国去了。于是，齐桓公率兵继续追赶，去攻打孤竹国。

齐国军队胜利了，但是，这场战争打得很艰苦，战争是从春天开始的，直到冬天才结束。等回国时，沿途景物，山川草木全都变样了。齐国军队来时，正是花红草绿，道路分明，现在呢，沿途只是一片荒草，无法辨别回去的道路。

齐军的将士们都很着急，齐桓公派出几支队伍，分头去寻找出路；可是，派出的人马转来转去，还是找不到出路。这时齐军已经乱成了一团。在这处境非常危险的情况下，管仲站出来，向齐桓公建议说：

"狗离开家了，自己能找路回来，马也有这种本领，老马走过的路，它都能记住的。大王，我们就用老马带路吧。"

齐桓公兴奋地说：

"这个建议太好了，现在让我们选匹老马在前边领路吧。"

齐军整顿好队伍，解开几匹老马的缰绳，让它们自己随意行走，大队人马在后面跟随。转来转去，果然找到了回去的道路。

人们根据这个故事引申出"老马识途"这句成语，比喻很有经验的人，熟悉情况，遇事能起主导作用。

During the Spring and Autumn Period, a minority kingdom in the north called Shanrong invaded the State of Yan. The Yan thus appealed for assistance from the State of Qi. At the time, the State of Qi was strong and mighty. In accordance with provisions of a treaty, Qi Huangong, the king of Qi himself led the troops to the rescue. Among those accompanying the expedition was a famous minister of Qi, Guan Zhong.

The Qi army defeated the Kingdom of Shanrong, but the king of Shanrong escaped to the Kingdom of Guzhu. Thus Qi Huangong led his troops in hot pursuit to strike at Guzhu.

Once again the Qi army was victorious, but only at a bitter cost. The campaign had begun in spring and had lasted until winter. Thus, when it came time to return home, the Qi army found that the roads and landscape had entirely changed. When they came, there were bright flowers and luscious grasses, and clearly marked roads. Now everything was dead and brown, and there was no way to recognize the road home.

The Qi generals were quite worried, and Qi Huangong dispatched several contingents of troops to split up and search out the return road. But though the scouts wandered all about, the passage remained hidden from them. By this time the Qi camp was thrown into disarray. In the midst of the chaos and danger, Guan Zhong stepped forth and addressed the king, "When a dog leaves its home, it can always find its way back. A horse also possesses the same ability. An old horse will remember a road it has traveled. Your Majesty, let us use an old horse to lead us."

The king said eagerly, "This is an excellent suggestion. Let us now choose an old horse to place in the front."

The army was consolidated and several old horses were unhitched and allowed to roam freely with the troops behind. Eventually the road home was found.

The term "an old horse knows the way" is used to describe one with experience or who, being familiar with a situation, has the ability to lead in a crisis.

买 椟 还 珠

mǎi dú huán zhū

(买, buy; 椟, casket; 还, return; 珠, pearl)

KEEP THE GLITTERING CASKET AND GIVE BACK THE PEARLS

古时候，有个楚国人，家里藏着几颗珍珠，想拿到郑国去卖。为了能卖个好价钱，他想出了一个办法。

珍珠是装在匣子里的，要是把匣子制作的精巧些，装饰得漂亮些，就会使珍珠显得特别名贵，一定能抬高珍珠的价格。于是，他精心制作了一个盛这些珍珠的匣子。

这个匣子是选用上等名贵的木材——木兰树作材料，样式也设计的很美观。匣子制成后，在它的四周用各色玉石镶嵌成美丽的图案，把它装饰得非常美观漂亮。然后再用贵重的香料把它熏得香味扑鼻。最后，他把珍珠放在这个匣子里面。

这个楚国人来到郑国市场上，把盛着珍珠的匣子摆在摊子上，果然吸引来很多顾客。大家都称赞这匣子精美漂亮。一个郑国人也被这个匣子迷住了，向卖珠人提出要买它，他出的价钱比这些珍珠的价钱还高。当场如数付钱。

郑国人把木匣拿在手中左瞧右看的，非常喜爱，连声说："盒子作得太精美、太好看了。"

看了许久，他才打开木匣，将匣子里的珍珠倒出来。楚国人还以为他更喜爱珍珠呢。可是万万没有想到，这个郑国人以为是卖珠人把珍珠遗忘在这里了，所以，将珍珠还给卖珠人，提着木匣高兴地走了。卖珠的楚国人只卖掉了装珍珠的盒子，却没有卖掉珍珠。

周围的顾客也感到奇怪，议论着这个郑国人没有鉴别的能力，不知道珍珠要比盒子贵重许多倍呢！

后来人们根据这个故事引申出"买椟还珠"这句成语，比喻没有眼光，缺乏鉴别事物的能力，只重表面，不顾实质。

In ancient times there was a man from the State of Chu who had several valuable pearls, which he took to the State of Zheng to sell. In order to get a better price, he formed a plan.

If an exquisite casket could be made to hold the pearls, it would lend an even more valuable appearance to the pearls and definitely raise their price. Therefore, he painstakingly began to build a little box to hold the pearls.

The casket was made out of the finest magnolia wood and designed in very eye-pleasing manner. Then it was encrusted with precious stones of all colors arranged in beautiful patterns. Then a valuable perfume was used to imbue the box with a fragrant aroma. Finally, he placed the pearls inside the casket.

Arriving in a Zheng marketplace, the man placed the casket on the table of a vending stall. As expected, it attracted many people, and everyone praised the fine workmanship and beauty of the casket. One local man was absolutely taken with the little box and offered to buy it. The figure he named was higher than the value of the pearls, and he paid it on the spot.

The man from Zheng held the casket in his hands, peering at it from all sides, totally enraptured. He said, "This box is so exquisite ... so beautiful!"

After admiring it for a long time, he finally opened it, and the pearls tumbled out. The Chu man thought that the man would like the pearls even more. However, the man thought the pearls were accidentally left there by the owner, so he scooped them up, gave them back, and happily carried off the casket. Thus the man from Chu succeeded only in selling the box he made to hold the pearls, not the pearls themselves!

The other customers were puzzled at the local man's lack of good judgment — didn't he know that the pearls were far more valuable than the box?

The idiom "keep the glittering casket and give back the pearls" is used as a metaphor for a lack of insight or judgment, only paying attention to the surface appearance of things without considering quality.

盲 人 摸 象

máng　　rén　　mō　　xiàng

（盲，blind；人，man；摸，feel；象，elephant）

A GROUP OF BLIND MEN
TRY TO SIZE UP AN ELEPHANT

从前，有一个国王养了许多大象。有一天，他坐在大象身上，带着手下人到外边游玩。走着走着，看见前边来了六个盲人。国王命手下人把他们都叫过来，对他们说：

"你们知道大象是什么样子吗？"

盲人们都说：

"我们是瞎子，不知道大象是什么样子。"

国王说：

"那你们就用手去摸摸看，然后再告诉我。"

大象被牵到他们的身边，盲人们赶紧围上去，各自从自己站的地方开始摸了。过了一会儿，他们都要向国王报告大象长的是什么样子。

国王说：

"不要着急，不要急，一个接一个地说。"

于是，摸到象的牙齿的盲人说：

"大象活像是一个又粗又长的大萝卜。"

"不对！"摸到大象耳朵的盲人说：

"大象像一只簸箕。"

"不对、不对！"摸到大象脚的矮盲人说：

"大象好象舂米的石臼，又圆又粗。"

"更不对了。"摸到大象脊背的高个子盲人连忙说：

"我猜大象是一张床。"

"你们都没有说对。"摸到大象肚皮的盲人自信地说：

"我仔细地摸了，大象是一个大瓦缸。"

"不，全都没有说对！"最后一个摸象鼻子的盲人满有把握地说：

"我摸了又摸，大象又长又细，仿佛是一根粗绳子。"

盲人们都说完了，便争论起来，你说他不对，他说你不对。国王最后说了：

"你们全没有说对啊！"

原来他们都仅仅摸到了大象的一部分，把摸到的一部分误认为全体了。

后来人们从这个故事归纳出"盲人摸象"这个成语，比喻那些了解事情只见局部，不见整体的人，会作出错误的判断。

Once upon a time there was a king who kept many elephants. One day, he sat atop an elephant and took his entourage to the countryside for an outing. After they had been on the road for a while, they saw six blind men on the side of the road. The king ordered them brought over to him, and he said, "Do you know what an elephant is like?"

The blind men answered, "We are blind and do not know what an elephant is like."

The king said, "Then come and let your hands see for you; feel the elephant and then tell me what you find."

The elephant was led over to the blind men and they quickly encircled it, each person standing in a different place, and began feeling it. After a moment they all started babbling to the king about the elephant.

The king said, "There's no rush, speak one at a time."

The blind man who had felt the elephant's tusks said, "An elephant is verily like a long, thick turnip."

"No!" cried the man who felt the elephant's ear. "An elephant is like a great fan!"

"No, no!" said the man who felt the elephant's foot. "An elephant is like a mortar for grinding rice, thick and round!"

"That's wider of the mark," said the tall man who felt the back of the elephant. "I guess an elephant is like a bed."

"You are all wrong," said the man who felt the skin of the elephant's belly. "I carefully felt it, and an elephant is like a great tile crock."

"No! Not one of you is right!" said the last man with utter confidence, who had felt the elephant's trunk. "An elephant is long and slender, much like a thick rope."

When the blind men finished speaking, they began arguing among themselves as to who was right. Finally the king cut in, "You are all wrong!"

132

Each man had only felt one part of the elephant, mistaking it for the whole.

The phrase "a group of blind men try to size up an elephant" is used to describe those who, by only understanding a part of something without looking at the whole, come up with a faulty judgment or conclusion.

盲 人 瞎 马

máng　rén　xiā　mǎ

(盲, blind; 人, man; 瞎, blind; 马, horse)

A BLIND MAN ON A BLIND HORSE

古时候，有几个文人在一起喝酒闲谈，大家都很高兴。这时有人提议，在座的每个人，各自用一句诗来说出一件最危险的事情，来助一下酒兴。

甲首先说了一句：

"矛头淘米剑为炊。"

这句诗的意思是说：用长矛的矛头淘米，用宝剑的剑尖拨火作饭，结果淘米箩和饭锅的底都会被戳破的，这是危险的事。

乙接着念一句：

"百岁老翁攀枯枝。"

这句诗的意思是说：有一位已经活到一百岁的老人，爬到干枯的树枝上了，这句诗比上一句更危险。

丙想了想，说出一句：

"井上辘轳卧婴儿。"

这句诗的意思是说：井口的辘轳上躺着一个婴儿，只要能滚动的辘轳一转，婴儿就掉进井里了，这当然是危险的。

甲和乙都称赞这句诗比自己说的处境更危险。

最后，文人丁也说了两句：

"盲人骑瞎马，夜半临深池。"

这两句诗的意思是说：一个瞎了眼睛的盲人，骑在一匹瞎了眼睛的马上，在漆黑的夜里，走到了深水池边。

大家都说，这太危险了，这太危险了，那个盲人肯定要掉下去的。

文人甲、乙、丙都一致称赞，这两句诗比我们说的好，比我们的强。

人们根据这个故事归纳出"盲人瞎马"这句成语。比喻乱闯瞎撞，非常危险。

Once there was a group of men sitting around drinking wine and chatting. Everyone was having a good time. Somebody made a suggestion that, to help along the rapture of the wine, each person should use one sentence to describe the most dangerous situation he could think of.

The first man said, "The rice is washed with a spearhead and the meal prepared with a blade."

His meaning was that if one uses a spear to wash rice and a sword to cook, the sieve and pot will be punctured, which is a dangerous situation.

The second man said, "An old man of a hundred years scales a withered branch."

The image of an elderly man climbing a dried and withered tree was more dangerous than the previous example.

The third thought and thought, then said, "On top of the well winch sleeps an infant."

Were a child sleeping thus to roll over or the winch to turn, the child would fall in the well. Extremely dangerous.

The first and second speakers both praised this line as being far more dangerous than their own.

The last man spoke, "A blind man astride a blind horse nears a deep pool in the darkness of the night."

Everyone agreed that this was very, very dangerous; the blind man was sure to fall in.

The other three unanimously extolled this line as being the best.

The line "a blind man on a blind horse" is taken from this story to mean one who rushes blindly into danger.

毛 遂 自 荐

mao suí zì jiàn

(毛遂, a man's name; 自, oneself; 荐, recommen)

OFFER ONE'S SERVICES AS MAO SUI DID

战国时期，那些有名望的王侯大臣们，家中都供养一批"门客"或称"食客"，为自己效劳。平时给主子出谋划策，研究问题。他们供养这么多人，也是培植自己的势力。其中，赵国国君的弟弟平原君赵胜的门客就有三千多人。

有一年，秦国出兵攻打赵国，并已经包围了都城邯郸。情况十分危急，赵国国君派平原君去楚国求援，并争取订立联合楚国共同抵抗秦国的盟约。

平原君准备带上二十名能文能武的人当助手，一同去楚国，便在三千名门客中挑选。但是，挑来选去最后只选中了十九名，还差一名怎么也选不出来了。正在这时，一位名叫毛遂的门客，自我推荐地说：

"听说还缺一名助手，就让我跟您到楚国去吧。"

平原君还不认识他，便问：

"先生到我这里有多长时间了？"

毛遂回答："三年了。"

平原君说道：

"人若是有才能、有本事，就如同锥子放在布袋里，那锥尖会露出来的。你到我这里三年了，从来没有人提到你啊？可见你没有多大本事。你不能随我去，还是留在家里吧。"

毛遂急忙说：

"以前若是把我放在布袋里，锥尖会露出来的。现在我正想请您将我放在布袋里，看看我到底怎么样。"

平原君听毛遂的话有些道理，就勉强同意带他去谈判。先选出的那些人，认为毛遂没有多大作用，所以，都瞧不起他。

平原君率人到楚国后，与楚国谈判。他们向楚王反复说明联合抗秦的好处。由于当时秦国太强大，楚国不敢同秦国对抗，所以，没有答应签订盟约，更谈不上出兵援救赵国了。赵国同楚国的谈判僵持下来，没有结果。

正在关键时刻，毛遂挺身而出，以他的机智勇敢说服了楚王，答应马上出兵援助赵国，并签订了联合抗秦的盟约。

后来人们根据这个故事引申出"毛遂自荐"这句成语，比喻不经过别人介绍，没有人邀请，自告奋勇，自己推荐自己。

During the Warring States Period, all the kings and dukes and high ministers each kept a retinue of guests at their homes, and whose services they kept at hand. Commonly, these guests would propose plans or discuss problems. By supporting these people, the aristocracy could also cultivate their own power. One of these aristocrats was Lord Ping Yuan of the State of Zhao, who supported over three thousand persons in his household.

One year, the State of Qin sent troops to attack Zhao and surrounded the capital of Handan. With a crisis at hand, the king of Zhao dispatched Lord Ping Yuan to the State of Chu to ask for assistance and to try to wrest a treaty from Chu that would unite them with Zhao against Qin.

To accompany him to Chu, Lord Ping Yuan decided to select from among his three thousand retainers twenty advisors well versed in both civil and military affairs. But after a grueling selection process, there were only nineteen persons, the twentieth remaining undecided. At this point, a man named Mao Sui stepped forward and in a self-recommendation, said, "I hear you are short one assistant. Please allow myself to accompany Your Lordship to Chu."

Lord Ping Yuan did not recognize him and asked, "How long has the gentleman stayed here?"

Mao Sui answered, "Three years."

The lord said, "If a man has talent, he is like an awl placed in a cloth bag: the point always sticks out. You have been at my residence for three years, yet I have not heard of you before. It is clear you have no special skill. You shall remain here."

But Mao Sui quickly replied, "If I had had the opportunity to be placed in a cloth sack, my point would surely have stuck out. Now I am pleading with Your Lordship to give me that opportunity and see how I fare."

Lord Ping Yuan felt there was some truth to Mao Sui's

words, and reluctantly agreed to take him along to the negotiations. The others who had been selected felt that Mao Sui could make no special contribution, and so looked down on him.

After arriving in Chu, Lord Ping Yuan and his advisors began discussions. Again and again they extorted the king of Chu to ally with them against Qin. But because at that time Qin was very powerful, Chu was unwilling to offer opposition. Not only would he not sign a treaty, he wouldn't even discuss sending troops to the aid of Zhao. The negotiations were stalled, with no result.

Just at the crucial moment, Mao Sui stepped forward bravely. He won over the king of Chu with resourceful and courageous words. The king promised to immediately dispatch troops to rescue Zhao and agreed to form an alliance against Qin.

The idiom "offer one's services as Mao Sui did" is used to describe those who volunteer or recommend themselves without introduction or invitation.

名 落 孙 山

míng luò sūn shān

(名, rank; 落, fall behind; 孙山, a man's name)

FALL BEHIND SUN SHAN

古时候有个读书人，名叫孙山。他很会说话，并很诙谐幽默，别人叫他"滑稽才子"。

有一年秋天，他到省城参加举人考试，临行前，邻居有位老人同他的儿子来了，请孙山带他的儿子一起去投考，以便互相有个照应，孙山一口答应了。

两人来到省城，报名后，很快就参加了考试。

过些天，考试发榜了。那天在大榜前挤了好多考生，都在寻找自己的名字。孙山也挤在人群中，昂着头，瞪着眼睛一个个名字看下去，可是一直没有看见自己的名字。他感到很失望，正要离开时，突然在大榜上名单最后发现了自己的名字，忙喊着：

"我中了，我中了！"

高兴地转身要走，又想起再看看老人的儿子是否考取了，但始终没有见到他的名字。

孙山回到旅店，见到老人的儿子，知道他确实没有考取。孙山安慰他几句，当天就回家报喜去了。

孙山回家后，乡亲们都来看他，向他祝贺。邻居老人也来了，急切地问孙山：

"我的儿子考取了吗？"

孙山在众乡亲面前，不好意思直说，却风趣地吟了两句诗：

"解名尽处是孙山，贤郎更在孙山外。"

邻居老人开始还有些莫名其妙，稍一琢磨，老人明白了，就闷闷不乐地回家了。

这两句诗的意思是：榜上最后一个名字是我孙山，你儿子的名字还在我的后面呢，当然就是没有考取了。

后来人们从这个故事及这两句诗中引申出"名落孙山"这个成语，比喻考试没有被录取，或比喻考试不及格。

In ancient times there was a scholar named Sun Shan. He was a good speaker and fond of humor. Others called him the "scholar comedian."

One summer, he went to the provincial capital to take part in the imperial examinations. As he was about to set off, an elderly neighbor approached with his son and asked Sun Shan to take his son with him to take the exams so that they could look after one another. Sun Shan readily agreed.

The two men arrived in the capital, registered, and soon took the examinations.

After several days, the list of successful candidates in the exams was posted. Many people crowded around the list, looking for their own names. Sun Shan squeezed in the middle. Raising his head, he began scanning down the list in search of his name, but it failed to appear. Feeling disillusioned, he was just about to leave when he suddenly saw the last name on the list — his own! He cried out, "I made it! I made it!"

As he happily turned away, he suddenly remembered to look whether or not the old man's son had passed as well, but his name was not to be found.

Sun Shan returned to his inn where he saw his traveling companion, and knew for sure that he didn't pass. Sun Shan consoled him with a few words and that day set out for home with the good news.

When Sun Shan arrived home, all the villagers came to congratulate him. His old neighbor also came, and pressed him, "Did my son pass?"

Sun Shan was embarrassed to speak directly in front of the crowd, and so chanted a couple lines of humorous poetry:

"Last on the list was Sun Shan's name, the young man's after Sun Shan's came."

The old man was a bit mystified at first. But thinking it

over, he understood, and sadly went back home.

Of course, what Sun Shan meant was that his name was last on the list of successful candidates, and the old man's son's name came after his own; therefore, he did not pass.

Now the idiom "fall behind Sun Shan" is used as a metaphor for failing to be admitted or not passing an exam.

南 辕 北 辙

nán　yuán　běi　zhé

(南, south; 辕, a part of chariot, here refers to the chariot;
北, north; 辙, rut, here refers to the road)

TRY TO GO SOUTH
BY DRIVING THE CHARIOT NORTH

战国时期，有一个人住在魏国。

一天，他要到楚国去。楚国本来在魏国的南边，可是这个人坐着马车，硬是往北边赶车飞跑。

他的一个朋友见他迎面跑过来，便打招呼问：

"喂，老朋友，你到哪儿去呀？"

他高兴地回答说：

"我打算到楚国去！咱们回来见！"

朋友有些惊奇，便叫车停下来，提醒他说：

"楚国是在魏国的南面啊，为什么不朝南走，而是往北走呢？"

他自信地说：

"没关系，我的马是一匹良马，跑得很快呢！"

这位朋友仍然提醒他说：

"你的马虽然好，可是这不是去楚国的路呀。马跑得越快，不是离楚国越远了吗？"

他还是自信地说：

"没关系，我带的路费多。"

这位朋友还是提醒他说：

"这是两回事，你的路费多又有什么用呢？这不是去楚国的路呀！"

他仍然不听，坚持说：

"我的车夫赶车本领高。" 接着，说声"回来见！"就让车夫赶车走了。

他的朋友皱着眉头说：

"唉！真是糊涂人。楚国在南面，他硬是往北跑，尽管他的马好，路费多，赶车的本领高，这些条件再好，离他要去的地方——楚国，只能是越跑越远呀！"

后来人们根据这个故事引申出"南辕北辙"这句成语，比喻行动和目的相反，目的是永远不会达到的。

During the Warring States Period, there was a man from the State of Wei.

One day, he wanted to go to the State of Chu. Chu was to the south of Wei, but this man got in his chariot and rushed off towards the north.

One of his friends saw him and ran over to greet him, asking, "Hey, old friend, where are you off to?"

The man merrily replied, "I'm going to Chu! See you when I get back!"

The friend wondered at this, and called the chariot to a halt. He reminded his friend, "The State of Chu is to the south of Wei. Why are you heading north?"

The man confidently replied, "No matter, this is a fine horse — he runs like the wind!"

The friend persisted, "Even though you have a good horse, you're not heading for Chu! The swifter your horse runs, the farther you'll be from Chu!"

Still assured, the man said, "It doesn't matter, I brought a lot of money for travel expenses."

The friend said, "These are two different things! What use is a lot of money? You're still not headed for Chu!"

The man spoke as though he hadn't heard, "My driver is very good, quite skilled in fact."

"I'll see you when I get back," he said, urging the driver forward.

The friend wrinkled his brow. "Ai! The poor guy's really confused. Chu is to the south, yet he insists on going north. Even with a good horse, a lot of money, and a skilled driver, he's just getting farther away from his goal — Chu!"

The idiom "try to go south by driving the chariot north" is used to describe those whose actions are in conflict with their goals, which remains forever unattainable.

囊 萤 映 雪

náng   yíng   yìng   xuě

（囊, bag; 萤, firefly; 映, reflect; 雪, snow）

READ BY THE LIGHT OF BAGGED FIREFLIES OR THE REFLECTED LIGHT OF SNOW

在我国晋朝,有两位著名学者,一句叫车胤,一名叫孙康。两人都出身穷苦家庭,小时候都不能入学堂读书,但都想学知识。他们白天要帮助父母劳动,到了晚上休息时才能挤出点时间读书。

晚上读书需要灯光照明,可是,家里连买灯油的钱都没有,怎么办呢?后来两人各自都想出了办法。

在夏天的一个夜晚,车胤偶然发现天空中的萤火虫,尾部闪出一亮一亮的光在空中飞来飞去。他猛然想到,把萤火虫捉来,利用萤光就可以在晚上读书了。于是,车胤找来一块很薄的白布,用它缝个口袋,把捉来的好多萤火虫装在白布袋里,到了晚上将袋子吊起来,借着袋中萤火虫微弱的亮光看书,刻苦攻读。

在冬天的夜里,孙康家里没有油灯不能读书了,他就躺在床上默默地背书。偶然向窗外望去,发现屋外的白雪将窗口映得很亮,屋外边比屋里还明亮。他便马上穿上衣服,坐在窗下,利用白雪反映出的微光发奋读书。

由于车胤和孙康刻苦学习,发奋读书,后来都成为晋朝有名的学者和政治家。

"囊萤映雪"这句成语,就是由车胤的"囊萤"和孙康的"映雪"顽强学习的故事而引申出来的,比喻刻苦读书的人,也是鼓励人们不要浪费时间,努力读书学习。

During the Jin Dynasty, there were two famous scholars, one named Che Yin, the other Sun Kang. Both men came from miserably poor families. Though unable to study in schools, they both desired to pursue knowledge. During the day they would help their parents work, and only during the evening rest period could they squeeze a bit of time to study.

Reading at night requires the light of a lamp, but their families were too poor to afford even lamp oil. What could they do? Both men thought of their own solution to the problem.

One summer evening, Che Yin noticed the flashing lights of fireflies bobbing in the air. He was suddenly inspired: he could catch some fireflies and use their light to read by at night. He scrounged up a piece of thin, white cloth and sewed it into a bag. Placing the captured fireflies into the bag, when evening came he hung it up and used the weak light of the fireflies to study.

During winter evenings, Sun Kang's family had no lamp to read by and he had to lie on the bed by the window quietly reciting books. One time he glanced out the window and suddenly noticed that the white snow outside was brighter than the room inside. He immediately threw on some clothes and sat beneath the window, using the feeble light reflected by the white snow to read.

Because of Che Yin's and Sun Kang's painstaking studies, they both later became scholars and politicians of great renown.

The phrase "read by the light of bagged fireflies or the reflected light of snow" of course refers to the hardships encountered by Che Yin and Sun Kang, and is used as a metaphor for studying hard or to encourage someone not to waste time that could be spent studying.

呕 心 沥 血

ǒu　　xīn　　lì　　xuè

(呕, vomit; 心, heart; 沥, shed; 血, blood)

SHED ONE'S HEART'S BLOOD

唐朝有一位著名诗人名叫李贺。他从小就很聪明好学,很有才华,七岁时就能写诗作文。李贺长大后,他的诗文写得更好了,已经是很有名的诗人。由于当时有些人嫉妒他的才学,使他不能进京参加进士的考试,以后就在家里,把自己的全部精力和心血投入到诗歌创作和研究上。

李贺创作诗歌是非常认真的,他为了写诗,有时衣袖磨破了,甚至头发也弄断不少。在他短短 27 岁的一生中,写出不少好诗,他的诗歌无论在当时还是后来都产生过很大的影响。

李贺并不是把自己关在屋子里写作,而是经常走出去,四处游览,观察社会,了解民情。

据说,他每天一早就骑上一头毛驴、背上书袋便外出了。在路上遇见好的题材,马上写成诗句,记在纸上,或者想到了什么好诗句,也立即写在纸上,均放到背袋里。回家后,再加工整理成诗篇,所以,李贺作诗并不是事先定好题目的。

李贺的身体不好,他的母亲见李贺每天这样劳累辛苦、勤奋写作,很担心他的身体健康。李贺每天晚上回家,母亲都让家人去看看背袋,如果背袋里记的诗句纸条太多了,就十分心疼地说:

"照这样下去,你的身体要累坏的,你是想要把心呕吐出来才算完事吗?"

同李贺同时代的文字家韩愈曾在一首诗中写道:

"刳肝以为纸,沥血以书辞。" 这两句诗的意思是把心肝挖出来当作纸,让血滴出来写文章。

后来人们根据李贺的这段事迹引申出"呕心沥血"这句成语,比喻人们写诗作文时穷思苦索,费尽心血。

There was a famous poet in the Tang Dynasty named Li He. From early on he displayed intelligence, a love of studying, and literary talent. He began writing poetry at the age of seven. As an adult, Li He's verses were even better and he established a name as a poet. Because some people were jealous of his ability, he was prevented from participating in the imperial examinations. As a result he just stayed at home, throwing all of his energies and passion into writing and researching poetry.

Li He was very serious about composing poetry — when he was writing, he would sometimes wear his sleeves through, and he even lost a lot of hair. In his short life of 27 years, he wrote many fine poems. Not only did his writings influence his time, but later generations as well.

Li He didn't always close himself up in his room writing, he went out often: traveling around, observing society, and trying to gain insight into condition of the people.

One legend has it that he would go out every morning atop a donkey, carrying his bookbag. If he happened to see something interesting on the road or think of something poetic, he would quickly capture it in a line of poetry, writing it down on paper and sticking it in his bookbag. Returning home, Li He would revise these verses, arranging them into proper poems.

Li He suffered from poor health. His mother, seeing her son exhausting himself daily with writing poems, was very worried about his physical condition. Each time Li He would return from one of his outings, his mother would make a family member to check his bookbag. If the bag contained many pieces of paper with poetry written on them, she would say with great concern, "If you go on like this you'll ruin your health. Will you be satisfied only when you cough up your own heart?"

A contemporary of Li He's, the literary great Han Yu, once wrote in a poem: "On paper once part of my flesh, I inscribe words of my blood."

Based on these accounts of Li He's actions was born the phrase "shed one's heart's blood," describing those who expend a great deal of effort on writing.

破 釜 沉 舟

pò   fǔ   chén   zhōu

(破, break; 釜, cauldron; 沉. sink; 舟, boat)

BREAK THE CAULDRONS
AND SINK THE BOATS

秦朝末年,秦始皇死后,他的儿子继承王位,称为秦二世。这时全国爆发农民起义,秦二世派兵镇压。随后又进攻赵国,把赵王围在赵国首都巨鹿。

赵王便派人向楚国求救,楚国国君楚怀王立即响应。便派宋义为上将军、项羽为副将,率大军前往巨鹿去援救赵国。

楚军行军到安阳,由于宋义害怕与秦军打仗,就驻扎下来不再前进。楚军停了好几天还不行动,副将项羽很是着急,便对宋义说:"救人如救火,我们还是起兵到巨鹿援助赵国吧。"

宋义说:

"不忙,先让秦军打赵军,等他们消耗了实力,打累了,我们再进兵也不晚。"

以后,项羽又多次劝说赶快起兵。宋义不耐烦地说:

"冲锋陷阵同敌人打仗,我不如你;但在帐篷里出谋划策,你就不如我了。你听我的,不要管那么多事。"

就这样楚军在安阳驻扎了40多天,宋义整天大吃大喝,再也不提援救赵国的事了。项羽非常气愤,在忍无可忍的情况下,把宋义杀死后,立即派一部军队先去巨鹿援助赵国,随后,他率领所有楚军过河北上。

过河后,项羽给士兵发够三天吃的干粮,然后下令把渡船全部沉掉,做饭锅都砸碎,岸边的营房全都烧光。项羽对将士们说:

"大家都看到了,退路是没有了,只有向前,与秦军决一死战,才能有生路的。大家要拿出拼命精神,不许后退一步,要战胜秦军。"

楚军到巨鹿前线,以一当十,个个都奋勇杀敌,死战到底,最后大败秦军,使赵国解了围。

后来人们根据这个故事引申出"破釜沉舟"这个成语,比喻只有前进,决不后退的决心,不惜牺牲一切以求胜利。

In the closing years of the Qin Dynasty, Qin Shihuang passed away and his son ascended the throne. At that time the whole nation erupted in peasant rebellions and the new Qin emperor mobilized troops to quell the chaos. Soon afterwards the Qin armies attacked the State of Zhao, encircling the Zhao capital of Julu.

The king of Zhao made an appeal to the State of Chu for assistance, to which the Chu ruler Chu Huaiwang promptly responded. With Song Yi as general and Xiang Yu as the assistant general, the armies set off for Julu.

The armies marched as far as Anyang, where, owing to Song Yi's reluctance to engage the Qin army, they made camp and advanced no further. After several days of non-activity, the assistant general Xiang Yu became anxious, saying to Song Yi, "Rescuing someone is like rushing to put out a fire. Why don't we mobilize our troops, march to Julu, and save Zhao?"

Song Yi replied, "There's no need for haste. We'll first let the Qin army attack the Zhao and wait for them to use up some energy. It won't be too late for us to attack."

Many times afterwards, Xiang Yu urged that they attack immediately. Song Yi became impatient and said, "In attacking the enemy lines, I'm no match for you, but in drawing up plans and strategies, you can't beat me. You do as I say and don't bother yourself with so many details."

The Chu army remained in Anyang for forty days during which Song Yi occupied himself with feasting and did not bring up the issue of rescuing Zhao again. In a rage, Xiang Yu killed Song Yi and immediately dispatched a regiment of troops to Julu to aid Zhao. Soon afterwards he led the rest of the army across the river.

After crossing the river, Xiang Yu issued each soldier three days of dry rations. He then ordered the boats sunk, the cooking pots smashed, and their quarters burned to the ground. He then said to his troops, "Everyone can see that we have no means of retreat. Only by advancing and engaging the Qin in a battle to the death will we have a road to life. Gird yourselves to defy death, do not give one step. Defeat the Qin army."

When the Chu arrived at the front lines of Julu they were outnumbered ten to one. Each and every man slew the enemy with great courage, fighting to the death. At last the Qin army was routed and the siege on Zhao lifted.

This story gave rise to the idiom "break the cauldrons and sink the boats," a metaphor for resolutely moving forward and obtaining victory at any cost.

杞 人 忧 天

qǐ rén yōu tiān

(杞, name of a kingdom; 人, man; 忧, worry; 天, sky)

LIKE THE MAN FROM QI WHO FEARED
THAT THE SKY MIGHT FALL

传说,古时候杞国有个人爱思考问题,但常常是胡思乱想。

有一天,他吃过中午饭,在院子里休息。当他抬头向天空遥望时,忽然想:

"要是天塌下来怎么办?"

当他低头往下看时,又忽然想:

"要是地陷下去怎么办?"

于是,他就坐不住了,"怎么办?"

他想,还是把家搬到一个安全的地方吧。可是又一想,哪儿都有天,哪儿都有地,到底到哪里去好啊?实在是无处安身了。

为这件"大事",急得他饭也吃不下,觉也睡不着,站也不是,坐也不是,他这样地忧虑着,使自己的身体一天天垮下来了。

邻居们知道他有这种想法,都觉得好笑,就开导他说:

"你别瞎操心了,天怎么能塌下来呢?天是什么,天就是一大团气,无处不有。你每天都要同它接触,从早上到晚上就生活在这里,你怎么担心它会掉下来呢?"

杞人听邻居这样解释觉得是有一定道理,但还是将信将疑,就进一步问:

"地会不会陷下去呢?"

邻居说:

"地是什么?地无非是堆积起来很厚很厚的泥土和石块,东西南北四面八方到处都有。你也是在地上走路、跑步、蹦跳呀。你担心地会塌陷下去这不是多余的吗?你呀,就是没事找事瞎担心。"

现在看来,邻居解释天地并不很科学,但这样一解释,杞人受到启发,才安心下来照常生活了。

后来人们根据这个故事引申出"杞人忧天"这句成语,现在用来比喻不必要或无根据的忧虑和担心。

Once upon a time there was a man from Qi who loved to ponder things, but who often confused himself by doing so.

One day, after eating lunch he took a rest in his courtyard. As he raised his head and gazed at the sky, he suddenly thought, "What if the sky falls down?"

Looking down at the ground, he thought, "What if the earth caved in?"

Afterwards, he couldn't sit still with worry: "What should I do?"

He thought about moving somewhere safer, but then realized that wherever he went there would be the sky and the earth. Where could he go? No place was out of harm's way.

He became so anxious that he couldn't eat, sleep, stand, or sit. Day by day his health worsened.

His neighbors were amused by his crazy ideas and tried to straighten him out:

"Don't worry yourself over nothing. How could the sky possible fall in? What is the sky? Just a huge mass of air. It permeates everywhere, and you come in contact with it every day. From morning till night you live in it, so how can you be worried that it will fall?"

The man felt that there was a certain logic to this explanation, but skeptically asked, "What about the earth collapsing?"

A neighbor said, "What is the earth? The earth is nothing but dirt and rocks piled up really thick. North, south, east, west: it goes off in every direction. You walk, run, and jump on the earth. Don't you think it's rather useless to worry about it caving in? You sure can make a fuss over nothing!"

Today, we can see that the neighbor's explanation wasn't very scientific, but it enlightened the man from Qi and allowed him to resume a carefree life.

The idiom "like the man from Qi who feared that the sky might fall" is used to describe one who holds a needless or groundless fear or worry.

曲 突 徙 薪

qǔ　　tū　　xī　　xīn

（曲，bend；突，chimney；徙，remove；薪，firewood）

BEND THE CHIMNEY AND REMOVE THE FUEL

从前有一个人名叫王二,是个木匠。有一天,他到朋友刘三家串门。到了中午,刘三留他吃午饭。刘三作饭炒菜时,王二发现刘家的灶上烟囱是笔直通房上的,一烧火,灶里的火星就飞出烟囱了。王二便说:

　　"你家的烟囱太直了,灶里的火星很容易飞出去,这可危险啊,容易引起火灾。还是把烟囱改成弯曲的,让它拐个弯,这样火星就不会跑出去了。还有,灶门口堆积的柴禾,也要搬远一点,不然也会失火的。"

　　刘三听后,不以为然地说:

　　"没有那么严重吧,这灶用了好长时间了,并没有失火出事呀。"

　　王二的提醒,没有引起刘三的注意。

　　几天后,刘三正在作饭时,果然他家失火了,烟囱冒出的火星把房顶烧了,灶旁的干柴也着火了。这可把刘三急坏了,马上呼叫:"救火!救火!"左右邻居听到后都赶来奋力抢救。经过大家的努力,这场大火很快就扑灭了。但是,有的邻居在救火中被烧伤了,刘三感到实在对不住邻居们。

　　又过了几天,刘三把家安置整理好,就大办酒席慰问和酬谢邻居。把参加救火的人一一都请来,救火中受了伤,烧焦了头发,碰破了头的请到上座,其余的人按出力大小一一就座,可是,刘三没有邀请事先警告过他的王二。

　　参加宴会的一个邻居对刘三说:

　　"你要是当初听了王二的忠告,就不会发生火灾了,今天也用不着请大家喝酒了。你把救火中受伤的人请入上座。如果论功请客的话,功劳最大的应该是王二,可是,你把他给忘记了,这可不对呀。"

　　刘三听后认为很对,马上让家人把王二请来,并且让他坐在上座。

　　后来人们根据这个故事引申出"曲突徙薪"这句成语,这个成语比喻对于可能发生的事故,事前要做好防备工作,以免发生灾祸。

Once upon a time there was a carpenter named Wang Er. One day he dropped in to visit his friend Liu San. At noon, Liu San invited him to lunch. As Liu San was cooking, Wang Er noticed that Liu's chimney stuck straight up out of the house. Each time a fire was lit, sparks would come flying out of the stove's chimney. Wang Er said, "Your chimney is too straight — it's easy for sparks to escape and that's dangerous because they could start a fire very easily. You really should bend the stovepipe at an angle to prevent the sparks from escaping. Also, you've got a lot of firewood stacked right by your stove. You should move it away a little bit, otherwise it might catch on fire."

Liu San objected, "It's not that serious. I've used this stove for ages and nothing's ever caught fire!"

Wang Er's reminder failed to grab the attention of Liu San.

Several days later, Liu San was cooking, and his house did catch on fire. Sparks out of his chimney caught the roof on fire, and the firewood by the stove also caught. In a panic, he yelled, "Fire! Fire!" The neighbors on both sides came rushing to the rescue. With everybody working together they quickly extinguished the blaze. However, some neighbors suffered burns in the process of putting out the fire. Liu San felt awful about this and was ashamed to face his neighbors.

After another few days, when Liu San had repaired and straightened out his house, he prepared a huge feast out of consolation and gratitude to his neighbors. Inviting all those who participated in the rescue, he placed those who suffered burns, singed their hair, or hit their heads to sit in the seats of honor. The others were seated according to their efforts in the fire. However, Liu San had not invited Wang Er, who had warned him of the danger in the first place.

One neighbor at the feast said to Liu San, "If you had listened to Wang Er's advice this fire wouldn't have happened, and this little party wouldn't have been necessary. You've honored those who were injured in the fire, but if you're going to invite people based on their merit, the one who contributed the most was Wang Er. Yet you've forgotten him completely. Surely that is not right."

Liu San felt these were true and had Wang Er brought over and placed in the seat of honor.

The idiom "bend the chimney and remove the fuel" has been drawn from this story to mean taking protective measures before an accident happens in order to prevent a disaster.

黔 驴 技 穷

qián   lú   jì   qióng

(黔, another name for Guizhou Province; 驴, donkey;
技, trick; 穷, exhausted)

THE GUIZHOU DONKEY HAS EXHAUSTED ITS TRICKS

古时候在中国的贵州省没有驴子，那里的人不知道驴子是什么样子的。

有一年，一个贵州人从外地买了一头驴子，跋山涉水，费了好大力气才把它运回来。到了贵州后，这里的人不知道驴子有什么用处，就把它放在山脚下，让它溜达、吃草。

有一天，从山上窜出一只老虎，到山下寻食来到这里。老虎忽然发现了这头驴子，被它吓呆了，心想：这么高大的身架，大头大嘴大耳朵，是什么东西？有多大本领？老虎以为驴子是什么神仙，不敢接近它，躲在树林里，瞪着两只大眼睛偷偷观察驴子的行动。过了好一阵子，老虎悄悄走出林子，慢慢地靠近驴子，细心打量着它，但还是猜不出这到底是什么怪物。

过了几天，老虎又怀着好奇的心情来这里观察驴子。这次它大胆地向前走了几步，这下子被驴子看见了。驴子抬起头，竖起耳朵，大叫起来。这一叫，吓得老虎调头拔腿就跑，跑了很远才停下来。老虎还以为驴子会吃掉它呢。

以后，老虎又经过几次试探，驴子见到它只是大吼大叫了几声罢了。老虎逐渐也听惯了，感到驴子没有太大的本领。

老虎的胆子越来越大，开始试着靠近驴子，最后壮着胆子，站在驴子的前边，驴子还是只有叫一叫。老虎更加放肆了，故意用爪子搔搔驴子、用身子碰撞驴子，最后，还绕到驴子身后咬它尾巴。这下驴子被惹急了，大叫着，抬起后蹄去踢老虎，老虎往后撤了一下，驴子就踢空了。

这一踢，老虎摸到了底，知道这个庞然大物原来就有这么点本事，于是，老虎发出吼声，纵身跳跃起来猛扑过去，张开嘴咬断驴子的喉咙，饱餐一顿。老虎把驴子吃掉，满意地离开，向山林走去。

以后人们根据这个故事引申出"黔驴技穷"这句成语，比喻外表很强大，实际本领不大，就是有限的本领也已经使用完了。

In ancient Guizhou, a province in southern China, there were no donkeys, and people didn't know what a donkey looked like.

One year, a Guizhou person bought a donkey abroad and, after braving mountains and fording rivers, managed to bring it back to Guizhou. Once in Guizhou, nobody knew of what use a donkey might be, and just let it roam in the foothills eating grass.

One day a tiger appeared in the hills and came down to look for food. Suddenly discovering the donkey, it stopped, stupefied. It thought, "What is this thing? Such a large frame! Such a large head! Such large lips! And such huge ears! What can it do?" Thinking the donkey to be some sort of supernatural being, the tiger was afraid to get near it. It hid in the trees and stealthily watched the donkey's every move. After a long while the tiger crept out of the forest and slowly approached the donkey. The tiger carefully sized the donkey up, but still couldn't figure out what kind of monster it really was.

After a few days, the tiger got curious again and returned to check out the donkey. This time he was bold enough to get closer to the donkey, but was spotted. Lifting up his head, the donkey pricked up his ears and brayed loudly. The sound startled the tiger so badly he picked himself up and bolted, not stopping until he was far away. The tiger had thought that the donkey was going to eat him.

The tiger made a few more exploratory forays, and each time the donkey just brayed loudly. The tiger gradually got used to this, and began to feel that there was nothing special about the donkey.

The tiger grew bolder and began to try to get even closer to the donkey. Finally plucking up his courage, he stood right in front of the donkey. The donkey only brayed. Emboldened, he batted at the donkey, and used his body to ram that of the donkey's. Finally, he ran around to the rear of the donkey and bit down on its tail. This stirred up the donkey, and with a loud bray, the donkey lifted up his hind legs to kick the tiger. The tiger darted back for an instant, and the donkey kicked empty air.

With this kick, the tiger knew that this was all this seemingly ferocious beast was capable of. With a mighty roar the tiger leaped forward and snapped the donkey's neck with his gaping jaws. Devouring the donkey, the tiger smugly departed, returning to the forest.

"The Guizhou donkey has exhausted its tricks" has been taken from this story to indicate someone who appears large and menacing but in actuality possesses no great ability and has already used up whatever ability they may have had.

孺 子 可 教

rú　　zǐ　　kě　　jiào

（孺子，child or young man；可，can；教，teach）

THE BOY IS WORTH TEACHING

古时候有个人名叫张良,是汉朝的政治家。在张良年轻时,他的国家韩国被秦国灭掉了,当时张良曾雇人刺杀秦始皇。但刺杀失败了,秦始皇到处搜查缉拿他,张良就在下邳这个地方隐蔽起来了。

有一天,张良出门散步,当他走到一座桥头时,见一位老人坐在那里。老人见张良走过来,把一只鞋子扔到桥下,对张良说:

"年轻人,我的鞋子掉在桥下了,去把它给我拾回来。"

张良先是一愣,他怎么用命令的口气呢?又一想,他这么大年纪了,就没有同他计较,马上到桥下,把鞋子给他捡上来。

老人把脚一伸,又说:"给我穿上!"张良心想:这个老人真是得寸进尺啊。既然已经把鞋子替他捡来,就替他穿上吧,于是,张良跪下来给他穿上了鞋。

老人穿上鞋,站了起来,看一眼张良就走了。张良见老人的举动有些惊奇,呆呆地望着他的背影。

老人走了一段路后,又转回来,对张良说:

"你这个年轻人还算懂事,可以培养教育的。过五天后,你在天亮时,到这里来见我。"

张良见老人有些古怪,不是普通人,希望能从老人那里学到一些本领。

到了第五天,张良一大清早就来到了桥头,只见老人已经先来了,正坐着等他呢。老人表现出生气的样子说:

"你这个年轻人比我老头子起来的还晚,过五天再来找我!"

张良只好回去。过了五天,天还没亮,张良就来到桥头,这次又是老人先到了。老人再次责备他,又让张良过五天后再到这里。

又过了五天,这一次张良没到半夜就来到桥头。这次老人还没有到。张良等了一会儿,老人提着灯笼才来。

老人见到张良后,满意地说:

"年轻人就应该是这样。"

之后,将一部《太公兵法》送给了张良。

此后,张良认真阅读这部书,反复钻研。终于帮助刘邦打败秦王朝,建立了汉朝。张良成为开国功臣。

人们根据这个故事引申出"孺子可教"这句成语,用于年长的人称赞年轻人有培养成材的前途。

In ancient times there was a statesman from the Han Dynasty named Zhang Liang. When he was younger, his country, the State of Han, was wiped out by the state of Qin. As a result, Zhang Liang hired someone to assassinate Qin Shihuang, the first emperor of China. The attempt failed however, and Qin Shihuang began searching everywhere for Zhang Liang. Thus Zhang Liang holed up in a place called Xiapi.

One day Zhang Liang was out walking when he came to a bridge and saw an old man sitting there. When the old man saw Zhang Liang approaching, he took off one shoe and threw it over the side of the bridge. Then he said, "Young man, my shoe has dropped off this bridge. Go get it and return it to me."

Zhang Liang was stunned at first: the old man sounded like he was issuing orders. Then he thought, "He is my elder, I can't very well get in a row with him," and scampered down and retrieved the shoe.

The old man stuck his foot out and said, "Put it on me!" Zhang Liang thought, "Give this old man an inch and he takes a foot!" Since Zhang Liang had already brought the shoe up for him, he figured he might put it on him as well. Zhang Liang knelt down and put the shoe on the old man's foot.

The old man stood up, glanced at Zhang Liang, and walked away. Zhang Liang was a little stricken by the old man's behavior, and silently watched his retreating back.

When the old man had traveled a distance, he turned around and said to Zhang Liang, "You're pretty intelligent, young man, and I think worthy of some training and education. In five days hence, meet me here at daybreak."

Zhang Liang thought the old man a bit funny, but quite extraordinary. He hoped he could learn something from him.

After five days, Zhang Liang went to the bridge at first daylight only to see the old man had already arrived and was sitting there waiting for him. Angrily the old man said, "You're so young yet you get up later than this old man! Come find me again in five days!"

Zhang Liang could only return home. After five days Zhang Liang went to the bridge before there was light in the sky and again the old man had arrived there first. The old man berated him once more and told him to return in five days.

After another five days Zhang Liang arrived at the bridge in the middle of the night. After a moment, the old man appeared, carrying a lantern. Upon seeing Zhang Liang there he said with satisfaction, "This is how youth should be."

He then handed Zhang Liang a volume entitled "The Art of War of Jiang Taigong".

From then on, Zhang Liang assiduously studied this text, reading it carefully over and over. In the end he finally assisted Liu Bang in overthrowing the Qin Dynasty and establishing the Han.

The idiom "the boy is worth teaching" has been drawn from this story to refer to an elder praising the educational prospects of a youngster.

入 木 三 分

rù　　mù　　sān　　fēn

(入, penetrate; 木, wood; 三, three;

分, unit of length, about one third of one centimeter)

THE HANDWRITING PENETRATES THE WOOD

东晋时候，中国有一位杰出的书法家，名叫王羲之。他的毛笔字写得非常好，对中国的书法艺术有很大的影响，所以被人们称为"书圣"。

王羲之受父亲的影响，从小就喜欢练字，七岁时就能写一手好字。稍长大了，就请求他的父亲正式教他书法。

父亲说："等长大了再教你吧。"

王羲之恳求着说："如果我长大了再学，那就太晚了，还是现在就教我吧。"

父亲见他的决心很大，便系统地教他书法。

王羲之每天都在练字，即使在休息的时候，也在想着写字，手也在衣襟上画着，时间久了，竟把衣襟都画破了。就是走路、吃饭，甚至睡觉，还不停地用手指练字，真是让"字"给迷住了。

有一天晚上，王羲之上床睡觉了，还在用手悬空写字。但一不留神竟画到妻子身上了，他的妻子开玩笑地说：

"怎么在人家身上画，你自己的身子没有啦！"

这句开玩笑的话，竟提醒了王羲之：要创造出具有自己风格、特点的书法来。

从这以后，他吸取了以前书法家的长处，创造出一种独特的书法艺术。他的字秀丽优美而又刚劲有力。

传说，有一次王羲之把几个字写在木板上，再拿给刻字木工照着雕刻。木工刻木时，竟发现他的笔迹已透入木板里有三分深了。后人就用这个传说，来形容王羲之书法笔力的强劲。

人们根据这个传说引申出"入木三分"这句成语。它多用来比喻说话、写文章道理非常深刻。

During the Eastern Jin Dynasty, China produced an outstanding calligrapher named Wang Xizhi. His works were extremely beautiful and had a great impact on China's calligraphic arts. Thus he has been called the "saint of calligraphy."

From childhood, Wang Xizhi was heavily influenced by his father. He loved to practice his writing, and when he was only seven he could produce decent samples. When he was a little older he asked his father to start formally teaching him calligraphy.

His father said, "Wait until you are older."

Pleading, Wang Xizhi said, "If I wait until I'm grown up to start studying, it'll be too late. Please start teaching me now."

His father saw that his determination was great and proceeded to systematically teach him calligraphy.

Wang Xizhi practiced writing every day. Even while resting, his mind was always turned towards writing, and his hand would trace the characters on his clothes; after a while, his clothing was worn through with holes. No matter if he was walking somewhere, eating, or even sleeping, his fingers were incessantly moving as if writing. He had simply become fascinated with characters.

One evening while he was in bed sleeping, his hand was tracing characters in the air. Accidentally he began writing on his wife's body. Laughing his wife said, "How come you write on other people but not on yourself?"

This was only a little joke, but it reminded Wang Xizhi of something: he should create a style of calligraphy that expressed himself and his own characteristics.

After this, he absorbed the strong traits of the famous calligraphers of the past and forged a unique style of his own. His characters were exquisite yet vigorous and forceful.

It is said that one time Wang Xizhi wrote several characters on a board and took it to a woodworker to have the characters inscribed in the wood. When the woodworker began carving, he discovered to his surprise that Wang Xizhi's handwriting had already penetrated the wood one centimeter. This anecdote describes the power of Wang Xizhi's brushstrokes.

The expression "the handwriting penetrates the wood" is based on this story to describe a piece of writing or a speech which is profound and powerful.

塞 翁 失 马

sài wēng shī mǎ

(塞, frontier; 翁, old man; 失, lose; 马, horse)

THE OLD FRONTIERSMAN LOSES HIS HORSE

从前，有一位老年人，带着一家人，住在北方边境的一个城关里。人们都称他"塞翁"。

边境的地方很辽阔，满地是野草，所以，塞翁养了好多马匹。

有一天，他家里的一匹白马不见了，找了好多天也没有找到。邻居们替他惋惜，都来安慰他，可是，塞翁并不着急，还满不在乎地说：

"这算不了什么，丢了马虽然受到了损失，但是，我认为这说不定还是一件好事呢。"

过了一个多月，塞翁丢的那匹白马突然跑回来了，还带回来一匹好马。左邻右舍知道塞翁得到了好马，都到他家来祝贺。塞翁表现得很平静，并不为此高兴。大家都感到有些奇怪："这老头怎么这样呢？"塞翁见大家疑惑，便说：

"这也算不了什么，白白得到一匹好马，说不定会给我招来一场灾祸呢！"

塞翁的儿子很喜欢骑马。有一天，他骑上这匹跟来的好马，由于这匹好马不熟悉新主人，乱蹬乱跑。结果，塞翁的儿子从马身上摔下来把大腿骨跌断了。邻居们知道塞翁的儿子受伤了都来安慰他。老人并不为此事着急，也不悲伤，又对大家说：

"这没有什么，虽然儿子腿摔断了，这未必不是一件好事呢！"

一年后，边境发生了战争，塞上的青年都应征入伍，上前线打仗，结果十有八九是战死在沙场上。只有塞翁的儿子因跛腿，不能参军打仗，保全了性命，父子平安无事。

后来人们根据这个故事引申出"塞翁失马"这句成语，比喻坏事可能变成好事，好事也可能变成坏事。

Once there was an old man who lived with his family outside the walls of a city along the northern frontier. People called him "the old frontiersman."

The area along the northern border was vast and broad, and wild grass filled the land. Thus, the old frontiersman raised many horses.

One day, a white horse of his was not to be found, even after several days of searching. His neigbors felt sorry for him and all came around to hearten him. But the old man was unperturbed, saying without a care, "What does this matter? Although I take a loss, I don't think that this is necessarily a bad thing."

More than a month went by when the old frontiersman's white horse suddenly came back, accompanied by another fine horse. The neighbors knew that he got a new horse and all came around to congratulate him. The old frontiersman was calm, refusing to be gladdened at the event. Everyone felt this was odd, and asked among themselves, "What's wrong with the old man?" The old frontiersman saw the doubt on everyone's face and said, "What does this amount to? So I got a free horse. Who knows, it might bring disaster!"

The old frontiersman's son loved to ride horses. But the new horse wasn't used to having a new master, and when the youngster tried to ride it, it ran around and bucked wildly. The old man's son fell off the horse and broke his thighbone. When the neighbors heard that the old frontiersman's son was injured, they all came to offer consolation. But the old man was not upset or woeful. He said to everyone, "What does this matter? Although my son fell and hurt himself, this still might be a good thing!"

A year later there was a war along the frontier and all the youth in the area were pressed into military service and sent into battle. Nine out of ten were killed in the battlefield. Because of his broken leg, only the old frontiersman's son was spared from fighting. Father and son were safe.

The expression, "the old frontiersman loses his horse" describes the possibility of good luck turning to bad, and of bad luck turning to good.

三 令 五 申

sān   lìng   wǔ   shēn

（三，three；令，order；五，five；申，state）

ISSUE ORDERS THREE TIMES AND
GIVE INSTRUCTIONS FIVE TIMES

春秋时期，有位著名的军事家名叫孙武。他根据春秋时期的战争经验，写成了《孙子兵法》十三篇。吴国的吴王也读过这部书，对孙武很赞赏，但是对他还不完全相信。

有一次，吴王召见孙武说：

"可不可以把你书上说的，用少量的军队实地试试？"

孙武说："可以。"

吴王又说："用一队妇女当士兵试着操练，行吗？"

孙武说："行。"

吴王便挑选了160名宫女，请孙武操练。

孙武把宫女分成两队，让吴王宠爱的两个妃子担任两队的队长。每人都发了一件武器，并详细讲明了操练的内容和要求。这时，孙武又让人搬出各种刑具，三番五次地讲明要遵守纪律，听从指挥。可是，下边列队的宫女们表现出漫不经心，极不耐烦的样子。

孙武开始操练了。

随后，击鼓传令：

"向右转！"

宫女们不但未向右转，反而在队长带动下都嘻嘻哈哈地大笑起来。吴王在看台上，见此场面也冷笑着。

孙武严肃地说：

"对操练的要求，你们可能还未听清楚；对击鼓传令，你们还不熟悉，这是我指挥官的过错。"

于是，他又把操练动作的要求反复地说了几遍，并再次宣布纪律。孙武第二次击鼓传令了：

"向左转！"

宫女们在队长带动下还是嬉笑不停，极不严肃，不认真地执行命令。

孙武大声说道：

"我一切都交待得清清楚楚了，你们仍然是不服从命令，不听从指挥，这是你们两个队长没有负起责任，还带头违反纪律。"

他说完，便不顾吴王说情命令手下人把两个妃子推出去杀了。

这样一来，宫女们都害怕了，训练时队伍整齐了，个个都遵守纪律，规规矩矩地按要求去做了。

吴王见孙武善于练兵、用兵，又执法严明，就任命他为大将军。从此，在孙武指挥下，吴国建成一支强大的军队。

During the Spring and Autumn Period there was a famous strategist named Sun Wu. According to his experiences in the battles of that time, he wrote the thirteen sections of "Sun Zi's Art of War". The king of the State of Wu read this text and praised Sun Wu while still holding some reservations towards him.

One time King Wu called for Sun Wu and asked him, "Would it be possible to demonstrate the things in book using just a small number of troops?"

Sun Wu said it would.

King Wu asked, "Could you use squads of women in your drills?"

Sun Wu said he could.

King Wu then selected 160 palace maidens and invited Sun Wu to train them.

Sun Wu separated the women into two squads, and made the king's two favorite concubines squad leaders. Each woman was assigned a weapon and given detailed instructions on the form and requirements of the drills. Then Sun Wu had various instruments of punishment brought out, and exhorted the women again and again to keep strict discipline and obey all instructions. However, the regimented women appeared indifferent and impatient.

Sun Wu began the drills.

A drum boomed and an order was given: "Right face!"

Not only did the women not turn to the right, but the squad leaders started everyone giggling. From his viewing platform, King Wu smiled wryly.

Sun Wu said seriously, "You may not have heard clearly the requirements of the drills; you are not familiar with the drum and the orders. This is the fault of me, as commander."

Therefore, he repeated several times the instructions and

movements of the drills, and once again made an announcement for discipline. Sun Wu struck the drum a second time: "Left face!"

The squad leaders once again set the whole group to laughing and couldn't seriously carry out the order.

Sun Wu said loudly, "I have explained everything clearly. You still do not obey orders, do not do as the instructer says. This is because the squad leaders have not fulfilled their responsibilities; in fact, they have instigated breaches of discipline."

When he finished speaking, in spite of the protestations of the king, he ordered the two concubines executed.

After this, the palace women were frightened into shape. During the exercises their ranks were neat and orderly, and each one was well-disciplined, obeying every order put forth.

King Wu saw that Sun Wu was expert at training and using troops. Moreover, he was a strict and impartial disciplinarian. King Wu made him a high general. From then on, under the direction of Sun Wu, the State of Wu formed a mighty army.

From this story the idiom "issue orders three times and give instructions five times" arose, meaning to repeatedly order or exhort.

三 人 成 虎

sān　rén　chéng　hù

(三, three; 人, man; 成, create; 虎, tiger)

THE TESTIMONY OF THREE MEN CREATES A TIGER IN THE MARKET

战国时期，国与国之间经常有战争，但也常相互订立盟约。有一年,魏国与赵国签订了友好盟约,为了能使双方都遵守盟约，按照盟约规定,双方都要把太子或重要皇亲送到对方国家做人质。魏王把自己的儿子送到赵国当人质,派亲信大臣庞葱陪同太子前往。

庞葱担心他走后,会有人说坏话,以后魏王不信任他。所以,在临行前婉转地对魏王说:

"大王,我有个问题请您指教,假若现在有人向您报告说,城里大街上跑来一只老虎,您相信吗?"

魏王不假思索地说:"我不相信,大白天的,大街上怎么可能跑出来大老虎呢。"

庞葱又接着问:

"假若两个人向您报告,大街上跑来了一只大老虎,您相信吗?"

魏王想了想说:

"如果两个人都这么说,我是半信半疑,我要进一步考虑考虑。"

庞葱又追问着:

"假若是三个人向您报告,都说城里大街上跑来一只大老虎,您相信吗?"

魏王说:"如果大家都是这么说,这事不会是假的,我会相信。"

庞葱进一步说:

"大王,大白天街上不可能出现老虎,这是很明显的事情,可是就因为是三个人都说了,您就相信了。现在我要陪太子去赵国邯郸了,邯郸离我国大梁要比王宫离大街远得多,我想背后议论我的可能不止三个人吧,到时,请大王能细心地考察。"

魏王点头说:

"这些我知道,你就放心地去吧。"

庞葱陪太子去赵国后,果然有人在魏王面前说他的坏话,开始魏王还不相信,继而怀疑,再后来说他坏话的人多了,魏王竟信以为真了。

当太子做人质期满回国后，魏王果然没有召见庞葱，以后也不再重用他了。

后来人们根据这个故事引申出"三人成虎"这句成语，比喻听别人的话要仔细分析考虑，不要盲从轻信。现在也用来比喻谣言一传再传，一再重复，会使人信以为真。

During the Warring States Period, states were always fighting with other states, but they also establish alliances. One year, the states of Wei and Zhao formed a treaty of friendship. To make the two sides stick to the agreement, each sent a prince or other important royal relation to the other side to be a hostage, as per the stipulations of the treaty. The king of Wei was sending his son to the State of Zhao, and was sending his trusted minister Pang Cong to accompany him.

Pang Cong was worried about leaving because he was afraid that others would say bad things about him and the king would lose trust in him. So just before departing, he tactfully said to the king, "Your Majesty, I have a problem for which I would like to ask your advice. Suppose that someone were to report to you now that a huge tiger was running loose in the streets of the city, would you believe him?"

The king thought for a moment and answered, "I would not believe it. How could there be a tiger on the city streets in the middle of the day?"

Pang Cong then asked, "Suppose <u>two</u> people came and reported that a tiger was loose in the streets. Would you believe the report?"

The king thought again, then said, "Were two people to report to me thus, I would half believe it and half doubt. I would need to think about it more."

Pang Cong persisted, "If <u>three</u> people reported a tiger loose in the streets, would you believe them?"

The king said, "If everybody said this, then it could not be false. I would believe them."

Pang Cong said, "O King, there is no way for a tiger to appear in the middle of the street in the middle of the day. This is quite obvious. But if three people say it so, you believe them. I am about to accompany the prince to the Zhao capital of Han-

191

dan. Handan is much farther from our own capital of Daliang than the palace is from the city streets. Those who would discuss me behind my back number more than three, I think. When that happens, I ask Your Majesty to make careful investigations of the claims."

The king nodded and said, "I am aware of this. You can go with your heart at ease."

As expected, when Pang Cong accompanied the prince to the State of Zhao, some people began slandering him to the king. At first the king did not believe them. But then he began to have doubts. Later, when more people began to say things, he finally believed them.

When the prince returned home, the king refused to see Pang Cong, and thereafter never used him for anything important.

The idiom "the testimony of three men creates a tiger in the market" later came to be used to teach people to consider carefully what others say, and not to take people's statements lightly. Now it is also used to describe a story that somehow gains credibility as it is passed on.

守 株 待 兔

shǒu zhū dài tù

（守，stand by；株，stump；待，wait；兔，hare）

WAIT BY A STUMP FOR A HARE

从前有个种田人，有一天，他正在田里干活，忽然看见一只兔子从远处惊慌地跑了过来，由于跑得过猛，一下子撞到田地旁边的树桩子上，脖子折断了，倒在地上。

种田人见到后，急忙放下锄头跑过来，将撞死的兔子拎起来。他太高兴了，没费一点力气，捡到一只又肥又大的野兔，今晚可以美美地吃上一顿了。还没等收工，他就拎着死兔子回家了。

刚一进门，种田人的妻子见他手里拎只死兔子，便笑着问：

"啊！这兔子是从哪里抓来的？"

种田人笑着说：

"这兔子不是抓的，是它送上门的。"

种田人把经过说了一遍。妻子听了乐得合不上嘴了。

随后，他的妻子给他做了一顿美味可口的兔子肉吃，还说：

"你能天天拎只兔子回来，我顿顿给你做好吃的。"

从此以后，这个种田人就丢下了锄头，放下了其他的农活，整天坐在树桩旁边，呆呆地等着，想再得到一只撞死的兔子。

时间一天天过去了，再也没有第二只兔子撞死在树桩上了。可是，他的田里已经长满了野草，还惹得大家笑话他。

后来人们根据这个故事引申出"守株待兔"这句成语，比喻不经过自己的努力，却想得到意外的收获。告诉人们做任何事情都不能存有侥幸心理。

Once upon a time there was a farmer. One day when he was out working in the fields, a hare came scared and running from afar. Because the hare was running crazily, it smacked into a tree stump sticking out of the ground, and broke its neck.

The farmer saw this and hurriedly dropped his hoe and ran over, picking up the hare. He was elated — without lifting a finger, he had got a large, fat, wild hare. He would have a feast tonight! Without bothering to wrap up his work, he carried the hare back home.

As soon as he walked in, the farmer's wife saw what he was holding and smiled, saying, "Ah! Where did you catch the rabbit?"

The farmer smiled back and said, "I didn't catch it, it was sent to us."

The farmer told his wife what had happened. She thought it was marvelous.

Soon after, the wife prepared a delicious rabbit dish and said, "If you can bring a rabbit home every day, I'll fix you something tasty for every meal."

From that point on, the farmer put away his farming implements and sat by the stump all day, every day, waiting for another rabbit to come along.

The days went by, but no second rabbit killed itself against the stump. However, his fields were already overgrown with weeds, and everyone laughed at him.

The idiom "wait by a stump for a hare" is a metaphor for wanting to obtain something without expending one's own effort. It teaches the principle of not trusting to luck in doing anything.

熟 能 生 巧

shú néng shēng qiǎo

(熟, practiced; 能, can; 生, produce; 巧, perfectness)

PRACTICE MAKES PERFECT

宋朝有个很出名的射箭能手，名叫陈尧咨，他的射箭技术很高，射出的箭能箭箭中目标，做到了百发百中。为此，大家都很敬佩他。陈尧咨因此有些飘飘然了，认为自己了不起，天下无敌手了。

有一天，陈尧咨在射箭场做射箭表演，有很多人来观看。他射出的箭果真是箭无虚发，百发百中，赢得了一片喝彩声。他本人也是洋洋得意。

可是在围观群众中有个卖油的老人却不以为然，不和大家一起叫好。老人的举动被陈尧咨看见了，不高兴地问老人：

"你会射箭吗？你看我的箭法怎么样？"

老人看一眼陈尧咨，便说：

"我是不会射箭。你射的还可以，但这不希罕，只不过是手法熟练而已。"

陈尧咨听后很是不满，故意刁难老人说：

"你敢轻视我，那你有什么本领，摆给大家看看。"

老人见他这么不虚心，便说：

"那好，你就仔细看着！"

于是，老人从担子上取出一只油葫芦，放在地上，并把一枚铜钱盖在葫芦口上，再取勺子舀了一勺油，然后将这勺油高高举起，往油葫芦里倒。只见倒出的油像一条线，穿过钱眼，直流到葫芦里，一勺油全倒光了，铜钱上却没有沾上一点油星。大家看后，都为老人高超的技术而喝彩叫好。

之后，老人对陈尧咨说：

"我倒油，没有什么了不起的，只不过干得多了，熟练罢了。"

陈尧咨听后连说：

"对、对，老人家说的有道理。"

从此，他谦虚多了，不再那么傲慢了。

后来人们根据这个故事引申出"熟能生巧"这句成语，比喻做任何事情只要肯下功夫，经常练习，反复实践，技巧熟练了，干起来就得心应手了。

During the Song Dynasty there was a famous marksman named Chen Yaozi. His shooting skill was quite remarkable, with 100 percent accuracy. Everyone admired and respected him, and Chen Yaozi grew a bit cocky. He considered himself pretty extraordinary, and felt that there was no one on earth who could match him.

One day, Chen Yaozi was giving an exhibition at the archery range, and many people came to watch. No arrow was shot in vain: each one struck the bull's-eye, drawing gasps of admiration from the crowd. Chen Yaozi himself became swollen with arrogance.

But in the middle of the crowd there was one old oil peddler who took exception, not cheering with the rest of the spectators. Chen Yaozi noticed this, and said testily to the old man, "Are you an archer? What do you think of my skills?"

The old man fixed an eye upon Chen Yaozi and said, "I cannot use a bow. You shoot pretty well, but that is nothing rare, just a matter of practice, that's all."

Chen Yaozi resented the old man's words, and deliberately teased him, saying, "You dare to belittle me. What skill do you have? Let everybody see!"

The old man saw how close-minded Chen Yaozi was, and said, "Very well. Watch carefully!"

Then the old man took a gourd for holding oil off his carrying pole. He placed a metal coin with a hole in the middle over the mouth of the gourd. Then he used a ladle to scoop up a measure of oil. Raising the ladle up high, he began to pour the oil into the gourd. When the oil was gone, not a drop had touched the coin. Everyone oohed and aahed at the old man's skill.

The old man said to Chen Yaozi, "My pouring oil isn't anything special, it's just that I've done it for a long time."

Chen Yaozi listened and said, "Yes, the old man has a point." After this incident, Chen Yaozi was much more modest.

Thus this story gave rise to the expression "practice makes perfect" meaning that if one works hard enough at something, one will gain proficiency in it.

螳 臂 当 车

tāng bì dāng chē

(螳, mantis; 臂, arm; 当, obstruct; 车, chariot)

A MANTIS TRYS TO OBSTRUCT A CHARIOT

春秋时期，有一次齐庄公乘坐马车去打猎。马车正在前行，走着走着，道路上有只小虫子向车轮扑来，只见它气冲冲地舞动着两只前腿，好象在挥动着两把大刀，阻挡车轮前进。

齐庄公看见这么小的虫子，竟敢同比它身子大好多倍的车轮搏斗。他马上命令车夫把车停住，问道：

"这是只什么虫子？有这么大的胆量。"

车夫回答说：

"这是一只螳螂，这种小虫子只知道向前冲，不知道往后退。它根本不衡量自己到底有多大的力量。你看，车辆距离很近了，马上就被辗着了，可是它仍站立不动，不让车辆前进。它往往轻视对手，真是不自量力。"

齐庄公仔细地看着螳螂，高兴地笑着说：

"好一个无敌的勇士，我们别伤害它吧。"

随后命令车夫把马车后退，再往路边靠一靠，让开了它。

后来人们根据这个故事引申出"螳臂挡车"这句成语，比喻那种不自量力的人。

During the Warring States Period, Qi Zhuanggong, the king of the State of Qi, was riding a chariot to go out hunting. As the chariot was moving forward, he discovered on the road a small insect that kept pouncing at the wheel. He could just see it furiously flailing its two front legs, as though it were waving two knives, in order to stop the chariot.

Qi Zhuanggong saw how such a small insect was taking on the vastly bigger chariot wheel. He quickly ordered the driver to halt.

"What kind of bug is this, to have such courage?" he asked.

The driver answered, "It is a mantis. It only knows attack and nothing of retreat. It basically doesn't know the limits of its own strength. Look, the chariot is already so close. The mantis was about to get run over, but it still stood its ground. It always underestimates its opponent while overrating itself."

Qi Zhuanggong carefully stared at the mantis, then smiled happily.

"What a brave warrior! We shall not hurt him," he said.

Qi Zhuanggong then ordered the chariot to back up and go around the little mantis.

Today, the phrase "a mantis trys to obstruct a chariot" is used to describe those who overrate their own abilities.

螳 螂 捕 蝉　黄 雀 在 后

táng láng bǔ chán huáng què zài hòu

（螳螂，mantis；捕，catch；蝉，cicada；
黄雀，a kind of bird；在，at；后，behind）

THE MANTIS STALKS THE CICADA, UNAWARE OF THE ORIOLE BEHIND

春秋时期,吴国的吴王准备攻打楚国。很多大臣都劝阻他不要打楚国,认为现在时机不成熟,有害无利,也没有胜利的把握。可是,吴王已经下定决心,并下命令说:"谁再敢阻挡我,立刻处死。"

这样一来,大臣们谁也不敢劝阻了。吴王有个青年侍卫官还想劝阻吴王不要出兵。他知道直说会被杀头的,便想出个劝阻的办法来。有一天早晨天刚亮,这个青年侍卫官就来到了吴王休息的王宫花园,他手拿一把弹弓,在树底下转来转去。第二天早晨又来到这里。第三天、第四天早晨也是这样转来转去。有人感到很奇怪,就把这事告诉了吴王。

第五天早晨,青年侍卫官又来了,吴王也来了,便问他:

"你一连三、四天早晨到花园来干什么?你的衣服都被露水浸湿了,这何苦呢?"

这时,青年侍卫官手拿弹弓,对吴王说:

"轻声点,大王您往树上看,您看,有一只蝉只顾着一边吸露水,一边在鸣叫,可是,它没有察觉到有一只螳螂躲在它身后,弯着前肢,想要捕捉它呢。"

吴王听了笑着说:

"螳螂捕蝉,这有什么希奇的。"

青年侍卫官又说:

"大王你再看,螳螂只是一心想着捕蝉,但它不知道,还有一只黄雀在它身后,正伸长着脖子、瞪着眼睛,想啄它呢。"

吴王说:"这又说明什么呢?"

青年侍卫官将手中的弹弓搭上泥丸对准黄雀,说:

"黄雀只想吃掉螳螂,却没想到我的弹丸正对准他呢。"他接着认真地说:

"蝉、螳螂、黄雀都只看到自己眼前的利益,没有想到自己身后的危险啊!"

吴王听到这里,猛然省悟了,明白了青年侍卫官的用意,取消了攻打楚国的决定。

后来人们根据这个故事引申出了"螳螂捕蝉,黄雀在后"这句成语,比喻目光短浅,只顾眼前利益,而不知后患会跟踪而来。

During the Spring and Autumn Period, the king of the State of Wu was preparing to attack the State of Chu. Many ministers exhorted him not to strike, believing that the time was not yet ripe, and that victory could not be assured. However, the king had made up his mind, and issued an order, saying, "Whoever dares to obstruct me will be immediately punished with death!"

Thus, none of his advisors dared to speak out against him. But the king had a young bodyguard who still felt he should warn the king against sending troops. He knew that to speak forthrightly would be to invite death, so he thought of a different way to get his message across.

One morning when the sky had just brightened, the young bodyguard went to the king's imperial garden. Holding a slingshot, he just kept walking around the trees. On the second day, he came again. On the third and fourth mornings he came, and continued to just walk around amongst the trees. People thought this was strange, and reported it to the king.

When the young guard came on the fifth morning, the king came as well, and asked him, "Why have you been coming to the garden these past several mornings? Your clothes are totally soaked by the morning dew. Is this worth the trouble?"

The young bodyguard lifted his slingshot and said to the king, "Quiet! Your Majesty, look, there, in that tree. There's a cicada absorbed simply in drinking a bit of dew and making its call. It is unaware that a mantis is behind it, bending its front legs in preparation for attack."

The king laughed and said, "A mantis stalking a cicada, what's odd about that?"

The young guard said, "If Your Majesty will look again, you will see that the mantis is so intent on catching the cicada that it is unaware of an oriole behind it that is stretching its long neck out to pluck it off the branch."

"So what does that mean?" the king asked.

The young bodyguard took aim at the oriole with his slingshot and a clay pellet and said, "The oriole is so intent on eating the mantis that it doesn't know that my slingshot is aimed right at it!"

He continued in earnest, "The cicada, the mantis, and the oriole are only aware of the immediate gain to themselves, and have not considered the danger which lurks just behind them!"

The king listened to this, and with a flash of insight, understood what the young guard meant. He then canceled his plans to invade Chu.

The idiom "the mantis stalks the cicada, unaware of the oriole behind," is used to describe those who are short-sighted, only paying attention to the immediate profit, unaware that future danger may follow.

铁 杵 成 针

tiě　　chǔ　　chéng　　zhēn

（铁，iron；杵，rod；成，become；针，needle）

GRIND AN IRON ROD INTO A NEEDLE

李白是我国唐代著名的大诗人。据说，他少年时代很贪玩，不用心读书。

有一天，李白在家里读书，读的文章总是背不熟。他有些不耐烦了，放下书本，溜出家门去玩了。

李白走到一条小河旁，看见一位老婆婆在磨什么东西。他来到旁边仔细一看，感到很惊奇，原来是在石头上磨一根大铁棒。

"老婆婆，你磨它作什么？"李白问。

"我要给我的女儿磨一根绣花针。老婆婆一边低头磨着，一边回答。

"什么！"李白听了越发感到惊奇，又问：

"这么粗的铁棒怎么能磨成绣花针呢？"

老婆婆严肃地说：

"孩子，你别看这铁棒很粗，只要我天天磨，就会越磨越细，功夫到了，就能磨成针的。"

李白觉得老婆婆说的很对，他很受感动。他给老婆婆深深鞠了一躬，就急忙回家了。

李白回家后，拿起刚放下的书本，一遍两遍地背诵，一段一段地记着，很快地背下来了。从此后，李白再也不贪玩了，发愤刻苦读书，后来成为著名诗人。

后来人们从这个故事引申出"铁杵成针"这句成语，用来勉励人们无论做任何艰苦事情，只要有毅力，肯下苦功夫，克服困难，就一定能做出成绩来。

Li Bai was one of the great poets of the Tang Dynasty. Legend has it that when he was young he was too fond of play and neglected his studies.

One day when he was home studying, he came across a passage that was particularly difficult to memorize. Impatiently, he put down his book and ran outside to play.

Li Bai came to the edge of a river, where he saw an old woman grinding something down. Coming to her side for a closer look, he was surprised to see she was rubbing an iron rod against a rock.

"Granny," Li Bai said, "what are you grinding that rod for?"

"I want to make an embroidery needle for my daughter," the old woman explained, still grinding on the rod with lowered head.

"What!" Li Bai exclaimed, even more surprised than before. "How can such a thick rod ever be ground down to a needle?"

The old woman answered him gravely, "Child, don't worry how thick the rod is. As long as I work every day, it will get thinner and thinner, until at last it becomes a needle."

The old woman's words rang true with Li Bai, and he was deeply moved by them. Bowing deeply to the old woman, he hurried back home. From then on, he studied furiously, and later became a great poet.

The phrase, "grind an iron rod into a needle" is now used to teach people that if they just have perseverance, anything can be accomplished.

外 强 中 干

wài qiáng zhōng gān

（外, outside; 强, strong; 中, inside; 干, weak）

OUTWARDLY STRONG BUT INWARDLY WEAK

春秋战国时期,有一年,秦国派兵攻打晋国。晋国接连吃败仗,晋国国君晋惠公不得不亲自率兵抵抗。

在出征时,晋惠公要叫人在他的战车上套上郑国出产的高大骏马,以显示自己的威风。大臣庆郑当时在旁边看到了,马上劝阻晋惠公,说:

"大王,打仗时历来都是用本国的马来驾战车的。虽然我国出产的马个头矮小些,但它适应水土,又熟悉道路;同时它也熟悉主人,听指挥,您也熟悉这些马,又会驾驭。而郑国的马刚刚到我国,外表看上去高大强壮,但打起仗来会失去常态,怯弱无力,血管膨胀,呼吸急促,乱踢乱叫。到那时,它不听指挥,就无法作战,您后悔就来不及了,请大王慎重考虑。"

可是,晋惠公并没有听大臣庆郑的忠告,他自信地说:

"我就不信我驾驭不了这匹马。快!快套上郑国的大马。"

最后,晋惠公坐在这匹马拉的战车上,领兵迎战秦国。

秦晋两军刚刚交战,郑国的马就惊慌起来,乱蹦乱跑,无法驾驭,一下子陷到泥坑里,进退都不行,晋惠公也无法指挥军队。

结果晋军大败,晋惠公被秦军捉住,当了俘虏。

后来人们根据这个故事引申出"外强中干"这句成语,比喻外表强壮,内里很虚弱。

One year during the Spring and Autumn Period, the State of Qin sent out troops to attack the State of Jin. After suffering a series of defeats, the king of Jin, Jin Huigong, was forced to lead his troops himself.

When it came time to set out, in order to present a regal appearance, the king called for his chariot to be fitted with an imposing steed brought from the State of Zheng. Qing Zheng, an advisor to the king, saw this, and immediately objected, saying, "O King, we have always used our own local horses in battle. Although our horses are a bit small, they are used to our land and are familiar with our roads. Moreover, they know their masters and obey commands. Your Majesty is also familiar with these horses, and are able to control them. But the horses from Zheng have only just arrived in our country. They are tall and strong on the surface, but in battle they will lose their normal demeanour, their wills will waver, and they will buck and whinny. Then they will not heed commands and will be unable to join the battle. But by then it will be too late for regrets. Please reconsider carefully, Your Majesty."

But Jin Huigong did not heed his Minister Qing Zheng's loyal advice, saying with confidence, "I do not believe that I cannot control this horse. Make quick and ready the horse!"

Finally, Jin Huigong seated himself in the chariot pulled by this horse, and led his troops to meet the Qin army in battle.

As the Qin and Jin armies clashed, the Zheng horse became frightened. Uncontrollable, it rushed into a quagmire where it became stuck, unable to move forward or back. The king was unable to command his troops.

In the end, the Jin were routed, and Jin Huigong became a prisoner of war of the Qin.

Today the idiom "outwardly strong but inwardly weak" refers to that which is strong in appearance but weak in reality.

亡 羊 补 牢

wáng yáng bǔ láo

（亡, lose；羊, sheep；补, mend；牢, fold）

MEND THE FOLD AFTER THE SHEEP IS LOST

古时候有个人,养了一圈羊。

一天早晨,他出去放羊,一数,羊怎么少了一只呢?再数还是少了一只。他在羊圈里仔细查看一下,才发现羊圈破了个窟窿。他想,一定是半夜里狼从这里钻进来,把羊叼走了。

邻居知道他家丢羊了,就来劝他说:

"赶快把羊圈修一修吧,堵上这个窟窿,不然狼还会来叼羊的。"

他却很安然地说:

"咳!羊已经被叼走了,还修羊圈干什么?"

他没有听别人的劝告。

第二天早上,他又出去放羊,再一数,怎么又少了一只呢,又数了一遍,还是少了一只。原来,狼又是从这个窟窿里钻进来,把羊叼走了。这才引起他的注意。他很后悔,自己不该不接受邻居的劝告。

养羊人立刻动手,找些砖头,和些泥巴,把这个窟窿堵上。他又全面检查一下,把羊圈修整得好好的。

从此,再没有狼来叼羊了。

邻居知道他已经修好了羊圈,便说:

"这就对了,丢失了羊再来补修羊圈,还不算晚呀。"

后来人们根据这个故事引申出"亡羊补牢"这句成语,比喻发现错误,及时总结教训,及时改正,进行补救,就能避免重犯错误。

Once there was a man who had a pen of sheep.

One morning when he went to put the flock out to pasture he noticed there was one sheep missing. He carefully examined the pen and discovered that a hole had been broken through. He thought, "A wolf definitely snuck in here during night and carried off a sheep."

When his neighbor heard the news, he came over and offered some advice: "You should hurry up and block up that hole, otherwise the wolf will come again and get another sheep."

But the man replied easily, "Aw! The sheep's already lost! What good will it do to fix the pen now?"

He wouldn't listen to anyone's advice.

The next day when he went to put the sheep out to pasture he discovered another sheep missing. Apparently the wolf had come in through the hole again and stolen another sheep. This finally got his attention. He regretted that he hadn't listened to his neighbor's advice.

He immediately set to work and patched the hole up with bricks and mortar. Looking over the pen again, he saw everything was in good repair.

After this, the wolf didn't get anymore sheep.

When the neighbor found out that he had fixed the hole, he said, "That's the way — if you lose a sheep, fix the pen, it's never too late."

Now the idiom "mend the fold after the sheep is lost" is a metaphor for making prompt action to correct one's mistakes, thus avoiding making bigger mistakes.

望 洋 兴 叹

wàng yáng xīng tán

(望, look; 洋, ocean; 兴, heave; 叹, sigh)

LAMENT ONE'S SMALLNESS BEFORE
THE GREAT OCEAN

传说，掌管黄河的神叫河伯。

每年秋天到来时，雨水很大，大河、小河的水都猛涨起来，全都源源不断地流入了黄河。使黄河里的水涨得满满的，水位急剧上升，使河面一天天宽阔起来，向对岸望去，连马、牛都分辨不清了。

黄河之神河伯见此景观非常高兴，认为自己了不起，沾沾自喜地说："看看，天下的壮观美景都集中在我身边，天底下谁能比我更伟大呢？"从此，河伯便想出去显示一下自己的威风。

于是，河伯得意洋洋地顺着黄河向东奔去，出了黄河口，来到了东海。这是他第一次见到大海，此时，他向四周望去，呵！一片汪洋，看不到边际，水连天，天连水，汹涌的波涛拍打着蓝天，呵！太壮观了。

河伯望着大海叹息着，对海神说：

"来到你这里，望着无边无际的大海，相比之下，我才觉得自己很渺小。常言说：越是知识学问少的人，越是以为自己很高明，别人比不上。实际上我就是这样的人。如果我盲目骄傲下去，就会永远被有知识有学问的人笑话啊！"

海神听了河伯的话，打比方说：

"我们不能同井底的青蛙谈论大海，因为它仅仅局限在小小的井中；我们也不能同夏天的虫子形容冰块，因为它受到季节的限制。同样，对见识少、学问浅的人，无法谈论高深的道理，你说，是这样吧。"

河伯听了海神的话，连连说：

"有道理，是这样。"

海神又说："现在你来到这里，通过亲身的体验，知道了自己见识少、学问浅，所以，我才同你谈论高深的道理了。"

后来，人们根据这个传说引申出"望洋兴叹"这句成语。原来的意思是指在伟大的事物面前感叹自己的渺小。现在用来比喻因力量不够或缺乏条件，无从着手而无可奈何。

Every year, when autumn arrives, there are great rains and all rivers big and small begin to rise, emptying their waters into the Yellow River. The level of the Yellow River swells, rising sharply. The surface of river expands so much that looking at the opposite bank, one cannot distinguish between horses and cows.

The deity who governs the Yellow River, He Bo, was always extremely pleased to see such a scene, thinking himself to be quite awesome. Full of self-satisfaction, he said, "Behold! All the magnificent sights under Heaven are all at my feet. Who in this world is able to compare with my greatness?" At this, He Bo set out to demonstrate his power.

He Bo followed the Yellow River, racing eastward until he came to the sea. This was the first time he'd seen the ocean. Everywhere he looked was a vast, boundless expanse of water. The water met the sky, and great rolling waves slapped at the blue sky. It was magnificent!

He Bo gazed at the ocean and sighed. Addressing the ocean god he said:

"Coming here and viewing this boundless ocean, I feel insignificant in comparison. It is said that those who do not possess much learning foolishly believe they are wise, and above others. In truth I am this kind of person. If I continue in blind arrogance, I will always be laughed at by those who know more than me."

The ocean god listened to He Bo and offered a metaphor:

"We cannot discuss the ocean with a frog in the bottom of a well, for it is confined to its small well; we cannot describe ice to a summer insect, because it is limited to that one season. Likewise, it is useless to discuss profound reasoning with unlearned people, don't you agree?"

He Bo said, "What you say makes sense."

The ocean god then said, "Coming here now, you have seen

for yourself that your experience is limited and your knowledge superficial. Only thus have I been able to discuss profound reasoning with you."

The original usage of the idiom "lament one's smallness before the great ocean" was to express one's insignificance before something grand and majestic. Now it is used as a metaphor for feeling helpless as a result of being unable to accomplish some task owing to insufficient strength or lack of conditions.

望 梅 止 渴

wàng　méi　zhǐ　kě

(望, look; 梅, plum; 止, quench; 渴, thirst)

QUENCH ONE'S THIRST
BY THINKING OF PLUMS

三国时期，有一位著名的政治家、军事家叫曹操。有一年夏天，他带兵赶路，来到一处干旱荒凉的地方。这时将士们口渴得嘴唇都干裂了，嗓子也很疼，一个个精疲力尽，几乎走不动了。曹操见到大家行军又累又渴，下令停止前进，就地休息。并派人四处找水源。

这里没有河、没有井，一点水也找不到。曹操又命令，让士兵就地挖井，挖了半天，也挖不出水来。

曹操明白，军队不能在这无水的地方久留。他很焦急，怎么办呢？曹操抬头往前看，忽然，想出一个办法。

曹操骑在马上，举着马鞭往前指着：

"啊！大家看呀！有解渴的东西了。"

将士们一听，个个精神起来，赶紧站起来向前看。曹操接着说：

"前边有一片梅林，现在梅子虽然还没完全成熟，但个个又甜又酸，咱们去吃梅子吧。"

将士们一听说是梅子，马上想到梅子的酸味，嘴里自然涌出了口水，顿时大家都觉得不太渴了，精神振作了，力气也就来了。曹操趁机会马上整顿好队伍继续前进，很快走出了这个地方。

后来人们根据这个故事引申出"望梅止渴"这句成语，比喻当愿望无法实现时，用不现实的联想来安慰自己。

During the Three Kingdoms period there was a famous statesman and military strategist named Cao Cao. One summer, while leading his troops on a pressing journey, they came to a dry and wasted land. The soldiers' lips became cracked and their throats were sore from lack of water. One by one they were sapped of their strength and were nearly unable to move. Cao Cao saw that everyone was wearying of the march, so he ordered a rest and dispatched people in every direction to search for water.

But this region had no rivers and no wells; not a drop of water was to be found. Cao Cao ordered his men to try digging for water, but none was found.

Cao Cao understood that his men should not stay for long in this waterless place. He became anxious and in need of a solution. Cao Cao raised his head and looked far ahead, and then he thought of an idea!

Astride his horse, Cao Cao pointed ahead with his horse-whip and shouted, "Hey! Look! There's something that can relieve our thirst!"

As the troops heard, they rose to their feet with hope and crowded forward to see what lay ahead.

Cao Cao continued, "There's a grove of plum trees ahead! The plums aren't quite yet ripe, they must be sweet and tart! Let's go get some plums!"

As soon as the soldiers heard "plums," they thought of the fruit's tartness, which started their mouths salivating. Soon they didn't feel all that thirsty, and life and energy stirred up in them. Cao Cao seized the opportunity and immediately ordered the troops and started them marching. Soon they had left the wasteland.

The idiom "quench one's thirst by thinking of plums" describes consoling oneself with imaginary thoughts in the face of a hope that cannot be achieved.

危 如 累 卵

wēi　rú　lěi　luǎn

(危, dangerous; 如, as; 累, pile; 卵, egg)

AS PRECARIOUS AS A PILE OF EGGS

春秋时期，晋国国君晋灵公为了个人享乐，正在修造一座高九层的楼台。 花费了大量的人力物力，三年了还没有建好。 不少大臣劝说晋灵公，停止修造楼台，别再干这种劳民伤财的事了。 可是，晋灵公就是不听，并说：

"我已决定了，以后再有人劝我，就一律杀头！"

不久，有个名叫荀息的大臣，要求见晋灵公。 晋灵公以为又是来劝阻他修楼台的呢，便准备了弓箭，打算把荀息射死。

荀息一见晋灵公满腔怒气地等着他，赶忙声明说：

"大王，最近我学了一点小技艺，想给您表演一下，解解闷。"

晋灵公这才有了笑容，放下手中的弓箭，便说：

"好，你表演吧，我看看你到底表演什么小技艺？"

荀息走到桌子旁，聚精会神地表演了。 他先拿出 12 个棋子，一颗颗摆好，又拿出九个鸡蛋，小心翼翼地在棋子上迭累鸡蛋。 他先是在棋子上摆五个，在第二层又迭累三个，第三层再迭累最后一个。 荀息就是这样，把鸡蛋颤颤悠悠地一层层垒完了。

旁边观看的人都很紧张，为荀息迭累鸡蛋捏一把汗。 晋灵公在观看表演时也是一样紧张，连大气也不敢出。 当荀息把最后一个鸡蛋勉强搁在堆尖上时，晋灵公直说：

"太危险啦！太危险啦！"

荀息已经表演完了。 他急忙说：

"这不算危险，还有比这更危险的呢！"

晋灵公马上便问：

"还有危险的！你再表演看看。"

荀息说：

"最危险的就是大王您建造的九层楼台，已经三年还未建完。为了建造楼台，农民无法耕地，妇女无法织布，田地荒了，布匹缺了，国库也空虚了。 邻国正要准备来侵略我国，国家将要灭亡了。 您说，这危险不危险?！"

晋灵公这才恍然大悟，便说：

"是太危险了。 是我造成了这么严重的损失，是我的过错。"

于是，晋灵公下令，停止修建楼台工程。

人们根据这个故事引申出"危如累卵"这句成语，常用来比喻情况非常危险。

During the Spring and Autumn Period, Jin Linggong, king of the State of Jin, decided to have a huge, nine-storey building constructed for his enjoyment. A vast amount of material and manpower was devoted to the project, but even after three years it was not finished. Many ministers advised Jin Linggong to put an end to the project, and pleaded with him not to continue with such wasteful and laborious things. However, the king did not listen. In fact, he said, "I have already decided to do this! If one more person attempts to advise me, I will have them executed!"

Not long after, a high minister named Xun Xi made a request to have an audience with the king. Jin Linggong thought that Xun Xi was coming to dissuade him from building his tower, so he readied a bow and arrow and planned to kill Xun Xi.

When Xun Xi saw that the king was waiting for him seething with rage, he quickly spoke to explain, "Your Majesty, I have learned a couple tricks lately. Allow me to demonstrate and relieve a bit of the tension."

Jin Linggong finally smiled and set down the bow and arrow. He said, "Fine. Perform. Let me see what little tricks you have learned."

Xun Xi approached a table and began concentrating on his demonstration. First he brought forth 12 round game pieces and arranged them together on the table. Then he held up nine eggs, and carefully began stacking them on top of the game pieces. Hands trembling, he piled them up level by level. First he put five eggs down, then three eggs on top of those, and finally one egg on top.

All those watching were nervous and breathless with tension. The king was equally tense watching the demonstration, not daring to breathe. As Xun Xi, with difficulty, put the final egg in place, Jin Linggong let out, "Too dangerous! Too dangerous!"

Xun Xi's demonstration was over. He quickly said, "This isn't so dangerous. There's something even more dangerous!"

The king immediately said, "More dangerous than this! Show me!"

Xun Xi said: "The most dangerous thing of all is that Your Majesty has spent three years building the nine-storeyed tower, and it still isn't finished. In order to build this tower, the peasants cannot till the land and the women cannot weave. The fields lie in waste, people's clothing are in tatters, and the treasury is empty. Our neighbors are preparing to invade us, and our country will be wiped out. What does Your Majesty think: Is this dangerous or not?"

Jin Linggong suddenly understood, and said, "Verily, this is too dangerous. I am the cause of these massive losses. I have been wrong."

Thereafter, the king ordered work on the tower stopped.

The idiom "as precarious as a pile of eggs" came from this story, and means an extremely precarious situation.

闻 鸡 起 舞

wén　　jī　　qǐ　　wǔ

(闻, hear; 鸡, rooster, here refers to the crow of the rooster; 起, rise; 舞, practice with the sword)

RISE AT COCK'S CROW AND PRACTICE
WITH THE SWORD

古时候晋国有一对好朋友，名叫刘琨和祖逖，两人年轻时同在一个司州衙内做文书工作。二人的感情很融洽，友谊很深厚，志向也相同，对当时腐败黑暗的社会现实很不满，共同立下大志，决心为国家做出一番事业来。

两人白天在同一案桌上办公，常常在一起议论国家大事，一谈就谈到很晚，还没谈完，有时就挤在一起睡觉。

有一次，祖逖和刘琨又在一起议论国家大事，谈论到很晚才睡觉。由于说的太兴奋了，祖逖躺在床上，怎么也睡不着觉，他还是在想，怎样才能练出本领，保卫国家和治理国家。到了半夜，忽然窗外传来了鸡叫的声音，祖逖受到启发，要抓紧时间，练出一身好本领为国家效力。于是，他忍不住推醒刘琨说：

"你听见鸡叫了吗？"

其实刘琨也没有睡觉。他说：

"人们都说半夜鸡叫是不吉利的。"

"不！"祖逖说：

"不能说这是不祥之兆。听到这声音我很振奋，它是催促我们，早起床到外边练武。"

这正合刘琨的心意。于是，二人马上起床取下床头的宝剑，两个热血青年在庭院里，舞刀弄剑，认真练武。从此后，不论是炎热的夏天，还是寒冷的冬天，也不论刮风还是下雨，每天早上一听到鸡叫，就立刻起床，到庭院练习武艺。

后来，祖逖当上了西晋的将军，他作战勇敢，打了很多胜仗，改复了不少的领土。

刘琨也当上了西晋的将军，当他得知祖逖打胜仗的消息，非常高兴。

以后人们根据这个故事引申出"闻鸡起舞"这句成语，比喻有志气的人抓紧时间发奋图强。

In the Jin Dynasty there were two very good friends named Liu Kun and Zu Ti. When they were young they both began working as clerks in the same government office. Feelings between the two were harmonious, their friendship ran deep, and they shared the same aspirations. Both were dissatisfied with the dark and corrupt social reality of the time, and both were determined to devote their careers to doing something for the country.

During the day the two worked at the same desk, and often discussed weighty matters of state, talks which often lasted well into the night. Sometimes they would just huddle together and sleep in the office.

One time, Zu Ti and Liu Kun got into another discussion and didn't get to bed until late. Zu Ti lay down on the bed, but because the discussion was so animated, he couldn't get to sleep. He was still thinking, "How can I develop some skills to protect and order my country?" Then, in the middle of the night, a cock's crow suddenly came through the window. Zu Ti was suddenly enlightened — if he worked hard, he could train himself to render service to his country. Unable to stand it, he nudged Liu Kun and said, "Did you hear the cock's crow?"

Liu Kun had been unable to sleep, either. He said, "People say it's bad luck when a cock crows at night."

"No," Zu Ti said, "you can't say this is a bad omen. Hearing this sound has inspired me. It's urging us to get out of bed and practice martial arts outside."

This was exactly what Liu Kun wanted to hear. The two jumped out of bed and grabbed their swords. The two intense young men went out into the courtyard and began practicing martial arts in earnest. From then on, whether it was the blistering summer or the frigid winter; no matter if it was windy or raining, every morning at cock's crow they immediately arose and began training.

Later, Zu Ti became a general of the Western Jin Dynasty. He was brave in battle and secured many victories and reclaimed much territory.

Liu Kun also became a general for the Western Jin Dynasty. When he heard about Zu Ti's victories, he was very pleased.

The idiom "rise at cock's crow and practice with the sword" is used to refer to someone who has high ambitions and drives to obtain them.

卧 薪 尝 胆

wò　　xīn　cháng　dǎn

(卧, lie; 薪, twigs and grass; 尝, taste; 胆, gall)

SLEEP ON BRUSHWOOD AND TASTE GALL

春秋时期，吴国和越国本是邻国却结下了怨仇，经常打仗。

有一年，越国被吴国打败了，越王勾践夫妇也被俘虏了。勾践被押回吴国后，被安排住在吴王父亲墓旁的石屋里，一边看墓，一边养马。

勾践在吴国受尽了凌辱，他为了能活着回国，表面上装出对吴王十分忠诚。三年后，吴王见勾践很顺从，就把他放回了越国。

勾践返回自己国家后，发愤图强，决心报仇雪恨。他为了不忘记耻辱，激励自己的斗志，在自己的住处挂一个苦胆，无论是坐着还是躺着，总是能看见。喝水和吃饭时，都要用舌头舔一舔、尝一尝苦味。晚上睡觉时，总是躺在柴草上。

勾践还同百姓一起参加农田劳动和养蚕。他的妻子也参加纺线织布。他们平时吃的饭菜很简单，穿的衣服也很朴素。对贫困人家，总是想法去救济。谁家有病人、谁家办丧事，他都去慰问。

在勾践领导下，经过十年发展生产，积聚力量，又经过十年练兵，越国强盛起来了，最后终于打败了吴国。

后来人们根据这段历史记载引申出"卧薪尝胆"这句成语，用以比喻刻苦自励，艰苦奋斗，发愤图强。

During the Spring and Autumn Period, the states of Wu and Yue were originally friendly neighbors, but then an enmity was begun and they often fought one another.

One year, Yue was defeated by Wu and the king of Yue, Gou Jian and his wife were taken prisoners of war. Gou Jian was escorted under armed guard back to Wu where he was forced to live in a stone hut next to the grave of the father of the king of Wu, and made to watch over the grave and raise horses.

Gou Jian suffered all kinds of humiliation, but in order that he might live to return to his country, he forced himself to act loyal to the king of Wu. After three years the king of Wu felt that Gou Jian was subservient to him, and thus allowed him to return to Yue.

When Gou Jian returned home he set about rebuilding his country, determined to avenge himself. To never allow himself to forget his humiliation, and to harden his fighting spirit, he hung a gallbladder in his room. Whether he was sitting or lying down, he could always see it. Whenever he ate or drank anything, he would lick it, tasting the bitter, bitter bile. At night, he slept on a pile of twigs and grass.

Gou Jian also participated with the common folk in doing farmwork and raising silkworms. His wife took up spinning and weaving. For meals he usually ate simple fare and his clothes were plain. He always thought of some way to help those who were poor. When somebody died or got sick, he would go offer consolences.

Under Gou Jian's leadership, after ten years of development and gathering strength, and after another ten years of training troops, the State of Yue once again became strong and powerful. Finally, it fought and defeated Wu.

Based on this historical tale, the idiom "sleep on brushwood and taste gall" means to undergo self-imposed hardships or struggle in order to obtain some goal.

天 衣 无 缝

tiān　yī　wú　fèng

（天，heaven；衣，clothes；无，no；缝，seam）

A SEAMLESS HEAVENLY ROBE

传说，古时候有个年轻人名叫郭翰。他很有学问，能写会画。

夏天的一个晚上，天气闷热，郭翰无法在屋里读书，便到院中乘凉。周围很安静。他躺在仰椅上，一边扇着扇子，一边凝视着天空。忽然间，他看到从天空中慢慢地飘落下来一朵白云，伴着一阵带香味的微风吹过，从天上飘下来的白云却是一位仙女，落在他身旁。

郭翰吃惊地站起来，不知说什么好，愣了半天，才问：

"你是人吗？怎么从天上下来呢？"

仙女说：

"我是仙女啊！"

郭翰对仙女从头到脚仔细打量着，发现她身上穿的华丽、漂亮的衣裳，一点缝合针线的痕迹都没有，是一块完整的绸缎制成的。

郭翰便惊奇地问：

"你的衣裳怎么找不到一点缝合的痕迹呢？"

仙女笑着回答说：

"我是天上的仙女，仙女的衣裳用不着针线缝制的，所以，你哪能找到衣缝呢。"

人们根据这个传说故事引申出"天衣无缝"这句成语。原义是说天上仙女的衣服没有衣缝，现在用来比喻事物的完好、自然、细微周密，找不到什么毛病、痕迹。

Legend has it that in ancient times there was a young man named Guo Han. He was very educated, and could both write and paint.

One stiflingly hot summer evening Guo Han couldn't bear to stay inside and study, so he went out into the courtyard to relax in the cool. The place was silent, and he lay down on a bench and gazed at the sky, fanning himself with a fan. Suddenly, he saw a white cloud slowly drifting down from the sky, accompanied by a fragrant breeze. The white cloud was actually a celestial maiden, who set down right next to him.

Guo Han jumped to his feet in surprise, not knowing what to say. He stared dumbfounded for a long time, then said, "Are you human? How did you come from the sky?"

The celestial maiden said, "I am a celestial maiden!"

Guo Han carefully looked the celestial maiden over from head to toe and discovered that her resplendent and beautiful robe had no trace of seam nor stitch; it was made from a single and complete piece of silk.

Guo Han said curiously, "How is it that your robe shows no seams?"

The heavenly maiden laughed and answered, "I am a celestial maiden from heaven, and our robes are not fashioned with threads and needles, so you will not find any seams!"

Thus arose the idiom "a seamless heavenly robe." It's original meaning was simply describing the clothing of the celestial maiden, but now has come to mean something that is perfect, natural, subtle, and free from flaw or mark.

悬 梁 刺 股

xuán   liáng   cì   gǔ

(悬, hang; 梁, beam; 刺, prod; 股, thigh)

TIE ONE'S HAIR TO A BEAM TO KEEP FROM NODDING OFF OR PROD ONESELF AWAKE WITH AN AWL IN THE THIGH

东汉时候，有个人名叫孙敬，是著名的政治家。他年轻时勤奋好学，非常喜欢读书学习。读书已成为他的嗜好，经常是关起门，独自一人不停地读书学习。每天从早到晚读书，常常废寝忘食。读书时间长，劳累了，还不休息。时间久了，疲倦得直打瞌睡。他怕影响自己的读书学习，就想出一个特别的办法。古时候，男子的头发留得很长。他就找一根绳子，一头牢牢地绑在房梁上，另一头系在自己的头发上。当他读书疲劳时打盹了，头一低，绳子就会牵住头发，这样会把头皮扯痛了，马上就清醒了，再继续读书学习。

这就是孙敬"悬梁"读书的故事。

战国时期，有一个人名叫苏秦，也是很出名的政治家。在年轻时，由于学问不多不深，曾到好些地方做事，都不受到重视。回家后，家人对他也很冷淡，瞧不起他。这对他刺激很大，所以，他下定决心，发愤读书。他常常读书到深夜，很疲倦，常打盹，直想睡觉。他也想出一个办法，准备一把锥子，一打瞌睡，就用锥子朝自己的大腿上刺一下。这样，猛然间感到疼痛，使自己清醒振作起来，再坚持读书学习。

这就是苏秦"刺股"读书的故事。

人们从孙敬和苏秦的读书故事引申出"悬梁刺股"这句成语，用来比喻发愤读书，刻苦学习的精神。他们这种努力学习的精神是好的，但他们所采用的方式方法不必效仿。

During the Eastern Han Dynasty there was a man named Sun Jing who was a famous statesman. When he was young he had a love of learning and studied assiduously. Studying had already become his hobby, and he would often close his door and study incessantly by himself. Every day from morning to night he would study, often forgetting to eat or sleep. Even after he grew tired from studying for a long time, he still would not rest. After too long, he would be so exhausted that he would just nod off. He was afraid that this would affect his studies, so he thought of a unique way to deal with it. In ancient China, men grew their hair very long. Sun Jing found a length of string and tied one end of it fast to a roofbeam and the other end to his hair. If he dropped off while studying, the string would yank his hair and stop his head from nodding. The pain of the skin on his head tearing would instantly bring him wide awake, and he would continue studying.

During the Warring States Period there was a man named Su Qin who also was a well-known statesman. When he was young, because he didn't have much learning, he held jobs in many different places, but was never put in any important position. After returning home, his family was very cold towards him and looked down on him. This provoked him greatly, and so he made up his mind to make a determined effort to study. He would often study late into the night. Exhausted, he would often begin to doze or fall asleep. He also thought of a way to prevent this. He would take an awl, and when he would start to fall asleep, he would jab himself in the leg. The abrupt pain would wake him up and invigorate him, and he could continue studying.

From the stories of Sun Jing and Su Qin comes the idiom "tie one's hair to a beam to keep from nodding off or prod oneself awake with an awl in the thigh," meaning to study assiduously or have a spirit of determination. Although this hardworking spirit is good, it is not necessary to emulate their study methods!

掩 耳 盗 铃

yǎn ěr dào líng

(掩, plug; 耳, ear; 盗, steal; 铃, bell)

PLUG ONE'S EARS WHILE STEALING A BELL

从前，有一个人很愚蠢又很自私，还有一个爱占小便宜的坏毛病。凡是他喜欢的东西，总是想尽办法把它弄到手，甚至去偷。

　　有一次，他看中了一户人家大门上挂的门铃铛。这只门铃铛制作得很精美、很好看，声音也很响亮。他想，怎样才能弄到手呢？最后决定：把它偷走。

　　他明明知道，只要用手去碰这个铃铛，就会"丁零"、"丁零"地响起来。门铃一响，耳朵就能听到铃铛的响声，有了响声，就会被人发觉了，那可就得不到铃了。怎么办呢？他忽然想出一个办法来。他认为，门铃一响，耳朵就会听见了，如果把自己的耳朵掩住，不是就听不见了吗？于是，他自作聪明地采用这个办法去偷门铃。

　　有一天晚上，他借着月光，蹑手蹑脚地来到这家大门前。他伸手向上摘门铃，但是，门铃挂的太高了，怎么也够不着，他只好扫兴地回来了。

　　回到家，他又想这怎么办呢？

　　他想叫邻居聋子一起去偷铃铛，踩着他的肩膀就能摘铃铛了，可是又怕人家不干，不和他一块偷东西。只好自己踩凳子摘铃铛吧。

　　第二天晚上，他带着凳子，又蹑手蹑脚地来到这家大门口。他踩着凳子，掩住自己的耳朵，便摘这只铃铛。谁知他刚碰到铃铛，铃铛响了，这家主人发觉了，就把他抓住了。因为别人的耳朵并没有掩住，仍然能够听到铃铛的响声。

　　后来人们根据这个故事引申出"掩耳盗铃"这句成语，比喻蠢人自己欺骗自己，但骗不了别人。也告诫人们不要做自欺欺人的蠢事。

Once upon a time, there was a very stupid and selfish man who had the rotten quality of loving to take advantage of people in little ways. If he liked something, he would always think of a way to get it, even if he had to steal it.

One time, he saw an exquisitely made bell hanging from someone's doorway. The bell was beautiful and made a lovely sound. He began to think of a way to get his hands on it. Finally he decided he would steal it.

He knew clearly that his hand only had to touch the bell to make it starting ringing. If the bell made noise, his ears would hear it and it would lead to his discovery. What to do? He suddenly thought of an idea. He thought, "If I touch the bell, my ears will hear the ringing. If I plug my ears, then I won't be able to hear it." Thus, thinking himself quite clever, he implemented his plan to steal the bell.

One evening, using the pale moonlight, he stealthily crept to the doorway. He reached up to pluck down the bell, but it was too high. No matter how he stretched, he couldn't reach it, and could only return in disappointment.

Back at home, he thought about what to do.

He thought about getting his deaf neighbor to help him steal the bell — he could reach the bell if he stood on his shoulders, but he was afraid the guy wouldn't go along with it. The best thing would be to stand on a stool to get the bell.

The second evening, he stole to the doorway carrying a stool. Stepping on the stool and plugging his ears, he grabbed the bell. Of course, as soon as he touched the bell, it rang, and he was discovered and caught by the house's owner.

The idiom "plug one's ears while stealing a bell" is used to mean a foolish person tricking himself but failing to trick others. It is an admonishment to people not to deceive themselves or others.

夜 郎 自 大

yè　　láng　　zì　　dà

（夜郎，name of a kingdom; 自大，be full of conceit）

THE LUDICROUS CONCEIT OF
THE KING OF YELANG

古时候，我国西南一带，有个夜郎国，首领名叫多同，自称为夜郎国国王。

由于这里山多，交通很不方便，与中原地区没有来往。在夜郎周围的十几个部落中，它是最大的。而国王多同从来没有到过别的地方，在他看来夜郎国是天底下最大的地方，最大的国家了。

有一次，多同带着手下人骑马去游玩。当他们来到一座山脚下，他仰望着高山说：

"看看这座山都顶到云彩了，这就是天底下最高的大山啦。"

他手下人也随声附和说：

"是，是，天下数这座大山最高。"

多同等人又往前走，并爬上一座山头。多同站在山上向四周望去。他骄傲地说：

"我的国土多么大，哪一个国家能比上夜郎国大？"

他手下人又随声附和着说：

"是，是，我们夜郎国是天底下最大的国家。"

多同等人又往前走，来到一条小河旁。多同又发表议论说：

"看看，这条大河多么宽、多么长，哪个国家有这么长的大河？"

他手下人仍然随声附和着说：

"是，是，这是天底下最长最大的河！"

多同非常自豪、非常骄傲，对周围的邻国总摆出一副大国的样子。

有一次，中原的汉朝派使臣寻找通往印度的道路，他们来到西南，路过夜郎国。使臣向国王多同介绍汉朝的情况，多同听后有些惊奇，有些不相信，就问使臣：

"你们汉朝有我们夜郎国大吗？"

使臣听后便笑了，说：

"汉朝现有好几十个州郡。你们夜郎国的地方还比不上汉朝的一个郡呢，你说哪个大呢？"

人们根据这个故事，引申出"夜郎自大"这句成语，比喻和讽刺那些知识浅薄，孤陋寡闻而盲目自大的人。

In ancient times, there was a kingdom in the southwest of China called Yelang. The leader of Yelang was named Duo Tong, and he called himself the king of Yelang.

Because Yelang was very mountainous, communications and travel were very difficult, and there was no contact with the central plains region of China. Surrounding Yelang were more than a dozen tribes, of which it was the largest. But the king of Yelang had never been to anywhere else, and he thought that Yelang was the biggest place, the greatest kingdom under heaven.

One time for amusement Duo Tong went horseriding with a small retinue. When they came to the foot of a mountain, Duo Tong gazed up at the mountain and said, "Look, this mountain reaches to the clouds. It must be the highest mountain in the world."

His retinue chimed in agreement, "Yes, yes, this mountain is tallest of all."

Duo Tong and his companions went forward and climbed the mountain. Duo Tong stood on the mountain and looked about him. Proudly he said, "My lands are so vast. What kingdom is greater than that of Yelang?"

Again his retinue echoed him, "Yes, yes, our Yelang is the greatest kingdom under the skies."

Duo Tong went forward again and came to the banks of a small river. The king commented again, "Look, this great river is so wide, so long. What other kingdom has a river so long and big?"

His companions still agreed with him, "Yes, yes, this is the largest and the longest river in the world!"

Duo Tong was full of pride and arrogance and put on big airs of importance to the neighboring kingdoms.

One time, an envoy was sent out from the Han Dynasty to find a road to India. When the envoy came to the southwest, he passed through the kingdom of Yelang. The envoy startled King Duo Tong with stories about the Han. The king was a bit skeptical and asked the envoy, "Is your Han larger than our Yelang?"

The envoy laughed and said, "The Han empire has dozens of prefectures. Your Yelang can't compare with just one of them. Which do you think is bigger?"

Thus the idiom "the ludicrous conceit of the king of Yelang" is used to mock those with little knowledge or learning who blindly exaggerate their own importance.

叶　公　好　龙

yè　　gōng　　hào　　lóng

（叶，a surname；公，lord；好，love；龙，dragon）

LORD YE'S LOVE OF DRAGONS

古时候，有一个人名叫叶子高。人们都称他为叶公。

叶公特别喜欢龙，在他居住的屋子里，墙壁上画着龙；屋里柱子上、梁上、门窗上都雕刻着龙；在他使用的杯、盘、碗、碟上都有龙的图案；他戴的帽子上镶着龙；他穿的衣服上绣着龙；他的被帐、座垫上也绣着龙的图案。

走入叶公的家里，就好像进入了一个龙的世界，到处都有龙的形象。这些龙张牙舞爪的就好像真的龙在云里飞翔着。

天上的真龙知道叶公这样喜欢龙，非常感动，便从天上下到地上来拜访他。

真龙下来了，一时间乌云滚滚，雷电交加。真龙来到叶公家里，把龙头伸进窗户探望，把尾巴拖在客厅里。

谁知叶公见到了真龙，吓得面无人色，浑身发抖，抱着头，转身逃跑了。

原来叶公所爱的只是画的、刻的假龙，而不是真的龙，说明他不是真的喜欢龙，只是表面上装腔作势。

后来人们根据这个故事引申出"叶公好龙"这句成语，比喻表面上爱好某些事物，但并非真正爱好它，甚至内心畏惧它。嘴上说的与心里想的不一致。

In ancient times there was a man named Ye Zigao. People called him Lord Ye.

Lord Ye loved dragons. On the walls of his residence were painted dragons. On the building's pillars, beams, doors and windows were carved dragons. On his cups, plates, bowls and saucers were pictures of dragons. On his hat was inlaid a dragon, on his clothes, blankets and cushions were sewed dragons.

Entering Lord Ye's home was like entering a world of dragons. Everywhere there were images of dragons. These dragons, baring their teeth and brandishing their claws, seemed to be circling in the clouds.

A real dragon in the heavens knew of Lord Ye's fancy, and was moved. It came down from the skies to pay him a visit.

As the dragon descended, dark clouds rolled and roiled, thunder roared and lightning flashed. Arriving at Lord Ye's house, the dragon stuck its head in the window and dragged its tail through the reception room.

Who would have guessed that when Lord Ye saw the dragon, the color drained out of his face, his whole body trembled with fear, and he turned and fled, holding his head.

Lord Ye only liked painted or carved dragons, not real ones. His professed love of dragons was actually a front for what he feared.

The idiom "Lord Ye's love of dragons" came to be used to describe one who pretends to like something but hates or fears it in reality.

一 鸣 惊 人

yì　　míng　　jīng　　rén

(一, one; 鸣, cry; 惊, amaze; 人, people)

ISSUE A CRY TO SHAKE THE WORLD

战国时期，齐威王作国君已经三年了，三年来，他什么事情都不管，就知道饮酒作乐，游山玩水。把国家的许多大事都推给大臣们处理，但他一见了大臣就讨厌，更不听大臣的劝说。周围的邻国都趁机侵犯齐国，夺走了不少地方。这时齐国上下，一片混乱，国家日益衰弱，面临灭亡的危险。

齐国文武大臣们心里很是着急，但又不敢再劝说齐威王。这时，有个大臣名叫淳于髡。此人长得很矮小，但他的口才极好，能说会道，而且非常风趣、诙谐。淳于髡看到国家已经到了快要灭亡的地步，决定冒着风险，去劝说齐威王。

他听说齐威王喜欢听近似谜语一类的隐语，就编了一段去见齐威王说：

"大王，我有一件事不明白，您是多才多艺，见识很广的人，请您指教。"

齐威王很感兴趣地问：

"什么事，请讲来听听？"

淳于髡见齐威王并不讨厌他，便说：

"听说我们国家有一只大鸟，就栖息在宫廷里，一住三年，既不飞也不叫。大王，您知道这是怎么回事吗？再猜猜这是什么鸟。"

齐威王一听心里就明白了，这是借隐语来讽喻我，用鸟来比喻我啊！于是，齐威王笑着说：

"我知道，这只大鸟要么就不飞，要飞就要冲破青天，飞的比天还高；要么就不鸣叫，如果要鸣叫就定会一鸣惊人。"

淳于髡赶忙哭着说：

"大王的指教十分正确，我们都等待着大鸟高飞和鸣叫。"

从此后，齐威王亲自管理国家，召集大臣们商讨国家大事，采取有力的措施，并整顿了国法军纪，又组织力量反击侵略。使齐国一天天强大起来。

后来人们根据这个故事引申出"一鸣惊人"这句成语，比喻平时不声不响的人，没有什么特殊表现，但突然一行动，就能干出十分惊人的成绩。

During the Warring States Period, the king of the State of Qi, Qi Weiwang had been in power three years. In those three years, he didn't give his attention to any serious matters, but instead drank, amused himself and traveled to the most beautiful places. He gave the most important affairs of state to his ministers, whose sight disgusted him. He refused to listen to any of their advice. All the neighboring states took advantage of the opportunity to violate Qi territory, seizing large tracts of land. All about, Qi was in chaos. The state daily grew weaker and faced the danger of being wiped out.

All of the civil and military officials of Qi were extremely anxious, but none dared to say anything to the king. At this time there was a minister named Chunyu Kun. Although he was very short, his speaking skills were admirable. Moreover, he had a good sense of humor and was jocular in conversation. Chunyu Kun was well aware of the state's plight and decided to brave the dangers and speak to the king.

He had heard that the king liked to hear riddles, enigmatic phrases and the like. So he thought one up and went to the king:

"Your Majesty, there is something I don't understand. You are clever and artful, a man of broad learning, and I ask your advice."

The king gleefully asked, "What is it? Please speak!"

Chunyu Kun saw that the king wasn't put off by him, and said, "I have heard that there is a bird in our country that roosts in the palace for three years at a time, but it does not fly or sing. Your Majesty, do you know why this is? Can you guess what bird this is?"

Qi Weiwang understood that the bird in this riddle was an allegory for himself. Smiling, he said, "I know, if this bird were to take flight, he would puncture the blue sky and soar higher than heaven; if he were to cry out, his cry would shake the world."

Chunyu Kun said, weeping, "Your Majesty's lesson is entirely correct. We are all waiting for the great bird to take flight and sing."

Afterwards, Qi Weiwang began personally handling affairs of state. He gathered his ministers together to discuss important issues and adopted forceful measures to deal with them. He rectified the laws of the state and military discipline and organized strength to repel foreign incursions. The State of Qi grew more powerful day by day.

The idiom "issue a cry to shake the world" is a metaphor for someone who is normally undistinguished but who, in a single motion, can produce achievements that astound the world.

一 鼓 作 气

yì　　gǔ　　zuò　　qì

(一鼓, first beat of the drum; 作, rouse; 气, courage)

GET SOMETHING DONE IN ONE EFFORT

春秋时期，强大的齐国出兵侵略弱小的鲁国，鲁国国君鲁庄公在曹刿的协助下率兵迎战。

在鲁国的长勺这个地方，鲁国军队与齐国大军相遇了，于是双方都摆开了阵势，准备打仗。

齐国军队仗着兵多、武器好，首先擂起战鼓，向鲁国军队发动进攻。齐军随着"咚咚"的战鼓声，勇猛冲杀过来。鲁庄公正准备下令擂鼓迎战时，曹刿赶忙劝阻：

"不行，等一等，还没到时候！"

齐军见鲁军没有反应，也就不敢再向前冲锋了。

过了一会儿，齐军见第一次进攻不行，便再次擂鼓发起进攻。鲁庄公又想擂鼓迎战，曹刿仍不同意，鲁军仍然坚守在自己的阵地上。

齐军第三次擂鼓进军，鲁军还是按兵不动。齐军三次进攻都不成，还以为鲁军力量弱小，不敢迎战。这时齐军士兵纷纷放下武器，找地方坐下来休息。

在齐军第三次擂鼓进攻之后，军心涣散的时候，曹刿马上对鲁庄公说：

"是时候了，现在我们可以进攻了。"鲁庄公立刻下令擂鼓出击。鲁军见到三次擂鼓时，齐军士兵骄傲的样子，都非常气愤，早已按捺不住了，个个摩拳擦掌。鲁军听到自己的"咚咚"鼓声，像潮水似的，奋勇冲杀出阵地。顿时，没有丝毫防备的齐军，被打得落花流水，四处逃窜。齐军大败，被赶出国境。

战斗结束后，鲁庄公问曹刿说：

"为什么要等到齐军擂三次进军鼓之后，我军才擂鼓出击呢？"

曹刿解释说：

"打仗主要靠士兵的勇气，往往是第一次擂鼓时，士兵的士气正旺盛；第二次擂鼓，士气就有些减弱了；第三次擂鼓时，士气就大为低落了。我们只擂第一次鼓，士气正鼓得饱满时，一鼓作气打败了齐军。"

后来人们根据这个故事引申出"一鼓作气"这个成语。比喻做事时，要鼓足劲头，勇往直前，一口气干到底，把它做完。

During the Spring and Autumn Period, the mighty State of Qi invaded the weak and tiny State of Lu. With the help of a man named Cao Gui, the king of Lu led his troops to battle.

The two armies met, arranged their battle formations, and prepared to fight.

The Qi troops were great in numbers and had fine weapons. Their war drums began to roll and they launched their assault at the Lu ranks. Accompanied by the "Boom! Boom!" of the drums, the Qi army boldly charged forward. As Lu Zhuanggong, the king of Lu was getting ready to give the order to strike the drums and meet the charge, Cao Gui hurriedly stopped him, saying, "No, wait. It is not yet time," he said.

When the Qi army saw that there was no reaction from the Lu, they didn't dare to advance any further.

After a moment, when the Qi army saw that its first charge didn't work, they again rolled the drums and rushed forward to attack. Lu Zhuanggong again wanted to strike the drums and meet the attack, but Cao Gui didn't agree, and the Lu army still steadfastly held their ground.

The Qi army charged a third time, but the Lu didn't so much as move. The Qi's three charges were all in vain, so they thought the Lu was too weak to come forth and meet them. Then, one by one, the Qi troops set down their weapons and looked for a place to sit and rest.

After the third charge, the fighting spirit of the Qi troops was sapped. Cao Gui said to Lu Zhuanggong, "Now is the time. We can attack." Immediately the king gave the order to roll the drums and strike. Watching the arrogance of the Qi troops during their three charges, the Lu soldiers were outraged. Barely able to control themselves, they were itching to get into battle. As soon as they heard the "Boom! Boom!" of their war drums, the Lu swept into the battlefield like the incoming tide. The Qi army, caught totally unprepared, was smashed to pieces, fleeing in all directions. The Qi were utterly routed and were pushed back beyond the border.

After the battle was over, Lu Zhuanggong asked Cao Gui, "Why did you wait until the Qi had charged three times before sending our own troops out?"

Cao Gui explained: "In battle, the most important thing is the fighting spirit of the troops. When the drum is first hit, the troops' morale is always at its highest. With the second drum roll, morale is reduced a little bit. Third time, morale falls greatly. We rolled the drums once, and our morale was at its fullest, and we defeated the Qi at one go."

The idiom "get something done in one effort" has been taken from this story to mean to go all out, advance bravely, and get something done in one stroke.

一叶障目　不见泰山

yī　yè　zhàng　mù　　bù　jiàn　tài　shān

(一, one; 叶, leaf; 障, shade; 目, eye;
不见, unable to see; 泰山, name of a great mountain)

A LEAF BEFORE THE EYE SHUTS OUT MT. TAI

古时候，在楚国有个穷书生，他闲居在家中，不务正业，总是胡思乱想，想意外地发财。

有一次，他读了一本书，书中说：螳螂捕蝉时，为了观察蝉的动静，掌握好捕捉的时机，总是靠树叶给它遮身隐蔽。穷书生读了这一段，信以为真，想入非非了。他想，要是能得到那片叶子，我也会隐身了。

于是，穷书生跑到外边，在大树下仰头寻找螳螂捕蝉的机会。等了好几天，他终于发现有一只螳螂正躲在树叶后，遮身隐蔽着，一下子举起双臂捕捉了蝉。穷书生急忙上树，去摘那片螳螂遮身的叶子。可是一不小心，那片叶子掉落下来了，和原先落在地上的树叶混在一起了。到底是哪片叶子能隐身呢？最后，他只好扫了不少落叶带回家去。

"你拿这些树叶做什么？"穷书生的妻子感到莫名其妙，问他。

穷书生笑着说："有好事！"说完就拿起一片叶子，遮住自己的眼睛问妻子：

"你能看见我吗？"

"能看见！"妻子如实地回答。

他又换了一片叶子，再问妻子：

"你看见我吗？"

"能看见！"妻子仍然如实回答。

穷书生试了一片又一片，妻子都说："能看见！"但他还不死心，还是一片片地遮住眼睛，一次次地问妻子。就这样试了好长时间，妻子有些不耐烦了。当穷书生又拿起一片叶子问她时，妻子不耐烦地说："看不见！"

"真的是看不见了吗？"

"真的！"

穷书生非常高兴，终于有了一片隐身的叶子了。

第二天，他带着这片树叶来到市场，看准一件好东西，一手拿着叶子，当着货主的面，拿走这件东西。一下子就被人家抓住，把他扭送到县衙门。

县官审明了他偷东西的前后过程，气得大骂道：

"你这个书呆子，一片叶子遮住你的眼睛，就连前面的高大的泰山也看不到了吗？"教训一顿后就把他放了。

后来人们根据这个笑话引申出"一叶障目，不见泰山"这句成语，比喻被细小的事情所蒙蔽，看不见全局和整体的情况。

In ancient times there was a poor scholar from Chu. He lived an idle life at home, never doing any proper work. He was always thinking up crazy ideas and ways to get rich quick.

One time, he read a book that said that when a praying mantis was trying to catch a cicada, it would first observe the cicada's movements to choose the perfect opportunity to strike, to this end, it would use a leaf to give itself cover, hiding its body. When the poor scholar read this, he took it to heart, his thoughts running wild. He thought, if only I could get hold of that leaf, I could be invisible.

The scholar ran outside and stood with head raised under a tree, searching for a mantis stalking a cicada. It was several days before he finally discovered a mantis that, hiding itself behind a leaf, snatched up a cicada with its two arms. The scholar quickly scrambled up the tree and plucked the leaf that the mantis had hid behind. But he was careless, and the leaf fell to the ground to mix with all the other leaves that had fallen from the tree. Which leaf was the one that could make him invisible? All he could do was to gather up a mass of leaves and take them home.

"What are you doing with all those leaves?" the poor scholar's wife asked him, puzzled.

The scholar laughed and said, "I have a good reason!" Holding up a leaf, he used it to cover his own eyes, then asked his wife, "Can you see me?"

"Yes!" the wife answered truthfully.

He held up another leaf, and asked again, "Can you see me?"

"Yes!" she honestly answered.

The poor scholar tried leaf after leaf, and each time his wife said she could see him. He didn't lose heart, though, holding up each one to cover his eyes, and each time asking his wife if she could see him. After this had gone on for some time, the wife became impatient. As the scholar held up another leaf and asked her if she could see him, she said, "No! I can't see you!"

"You really can't see me?" he asked.

"Really!"

The scholar was elated: finally he had found the leaf of invisibility!

The next day, he went to the market, taking his leaf along. He set his sights on something he wanted. Holding up his leaf, he went straight up to the merchant and took what he wanted. Of course he was caught in a flash and turned over the county authorities.

After the county magistrate inquired about the development of this theft, he angrily cursed the scholar:

"You stupid bookworm! With a leaf before your eyes, you couldn't see lofty Mt. Tai though it be right in front of your face!"

After getting a good reprimanding, the scholar was let go.

Thus the idiom "a leaf before the eye shuts out Mt. Tai" has come to mean that one is so taken with a trivial matter that one fails to see the greater picture.

疑 邻 偷 斧

yí lín tōu fǔ

(疑, suspect; 邻, neighbor; 偷, steal; 斧, axe)

SUSPECT THE NEIGHBOR OF STEALING AN AXE

从前有一个人，不知道什么时候丢了一把斧子。到底是丢了，还是被人偷去了呢？

他想：呵！会不会是邻居家的孩子偷去了，这个淘气的孩子可是常常在我家附近玩耍啊，于是，他就暗暗地处处留心这个孩子的一言一行、一举一动。

他觉得这孩子走路的样子象是偷斧子的，这孩子的脸色、表情也象是偷斧子的；就是从言谈声音上看还象是偷斧子的。他断定：没有错，准是这个小孩偷了斧子。

不久，他到山上去，在一棵树旁，无意间发现了自己丢掉的那把斧子，他高兴极了。这时，他才想起来，前几天上山打柴时，只顾捆树枝，忘记把斧子带回家了。

他有些后悔，不应该怀疑邻家的小孩。

回家后，再见到这个小孩时，他很喜欢，觉得这孩子走路的样子不象是偷斧子的；看看脸色、表情也不象是；再听听言谈声音更不象是偷斧子的。

他心想：这孩子很诚实可爱，决不会干出那种丢人的事。

后来人们根据这个故事引申出"疑邻偷斧"这句成语，比喻那些不注重事实根据，只凭主观臆断，对人、对事胡乱猜疑的人。

Once upon a time there was a man who misplaced his axe somewhere. But did he lose it or was it stolen?

He thought to himself, "Hmmm! Could the neighbor's kid have stolen it? That mischievous kid is always playing around my house." Thereafter, the man began to secretly watch the child's every move, every word.

He felt that when the boy walked, he looked like an axe thief; his facial expressions looked like those of an axe thief; his voice was like that of an axe thief. He had no doubts: this boy definitely stole his axe.

Not long after, the man went up into the mountains where, beside a tree, he stumbled across his lost axe. Of course he was delighted. Then he remembered that some time before he had come to the mountain to chop some firewood. Only thinking to bundle up the wood, he forgot his axe here when he returned home.

Then he felt a little regretful; he really shouldn't have suspected the neighbor's boy.

When he got back home, he was happy to see the little boy again. He felt that the boy didn't really walk like an axe thief, his face and expressions weren't those of an axe thief, and his voice didn't sound like an axe thief's.

He felt that such an honest and darling child couldn't possibly have done such a disgraceful thing.

The idiom "suspect the neighbor of stealing an axe" is used to describe those who, ignoring facts, rely on subjective assumptions to make suspicious judgements of people or situations.

有 志 竟 成

yǒu　zhì　jìng　chéng

（有，have; 志，will; 竟，in the end; 成，succeed）

WHERE THERE'S A WILL, THERE'S A WAY

东汉初年，有位著名将军名叫耿弇。 他原是个读书人，后来对军事发生了兴趣，常去看地方军队操练兵马，自己也常习武艺，并立志要当个军事家。

有一年，东汉光武帝刘秀在北方组织军队，耿弇参了军，后来打了不少胜仗，成为刘秀手下有名的将军。

有一次，刘秀派耿弇攻打地方军阀张步。 张步占据 12 个州郡，实力很强，兵马也多，根本没有把耿弇放在眼里，只派部下来迎战。 耿弇率军队勇敢作战，很快就攻下几座城池。 张步见他的部下打了败仗，便纠集了 20 万大军，亲自率兵反攻，想趁耿弇兵少又疲劳之机战胜他。

刘秀闻知耿弇同张步已经直接交战了，也亲自率兵来援助。这时，耿弇部下有人建议说：

"张步的兵力很强，等援军到了，再与张步决战吧。"

耿弇并不同意，他说：

"我们应当以战胜敌人来迎接皇上，怎么能把消灭敌人的任务留给皇上呢？"

耿弇说后，便带兵继续作战。 在战斗中，他的大腿被敌方飞箭射中了，耿弇毅然抽出宝剑将这支箭砍断，带伤继续指挥战斗。 双方打得很激烈，最后终于打败了张步的军队。

几天过后，刘秀率兵来到了，慰劳耿弇的部队，刘秀当众夸奖耿弇，说：

"以前你曾提出平定张步，我当时以为你的想法不太实际，难于成功。 现在，我才知道有志气的人，一定能把事情办成功的。"

后来人们根据这个故事引申出"有志竟成"这句成语，比喻人只要有坚定的志气，有决心战胜困难，最后就能把事情办成功。

During the beginning years of the Eastern Han Dynasty, there was a famous general named Geng Yan. Originally, he was a scholar, but later became interested in military affairs, often going to watch troops in training and practicing his own skill in martial arts. He was determined to become a military strategist.

One year, Emperor Guang Wu organized troops in the north, and Geng Yan entered the army. Later he fought many battles, becoming one of the emperor's most famous generals.

Once, the emperor dispatched Geng Yan to attack the regional warlord Zhang Bu. Zhang Bu was quite powerful, occupying 12 prefectures and having great numbers of troops and horses. He didn't think much of Geng Yan and sent a subordinate to do battle with him. Geng Yan led his troops bravely and quickly attacked several cities. Zhang Bu saw his subordinate defeated and massed 200,000 troops for a counterattack that he would personally lead. He hoped to take advantage of Geng Yan's inferior numbers and tired troops to beat him.

When the emperor heard that Geng Yan had already directly engaged Zhang Bu, he also personally led troops to come to his assistance. One of Geng Yan's subordinates suggested, "Zhang Bu's troop strength is very great. Let us wait for reinforcements before having it out with him."

Geng Yan disagreed. "We should greet the emperor with a defeat of the enemy. How can we leave the emperor with the task of wiping out the enemy?"

After having thus spoken, Geng Yan led his troops into battle again. During the fighting, an arrow struck Geng Yan in the thigh. Gritting his teeth, he used his sword to break off the shaft. Wounded, he continued the battle. The two sides fought with intensity, but finally Zhang Bu was defeated.

When the emperor arrived with his troops several days

later, he gave recognition to Geng Yan's feats, publicly praising him:

"When you first proposed supressing Zhang Bu, I thought the idea rather impractical, to be achieved only with much difficulty. Now I am aware that a man must have the will, and there will be nothing he cannot do."

Thus this story gave rise to the idiom "where there's a will, there's a way," meaning that if one just has the willpower to persist in overcoming difficulties, then anything can be accomplished.

余 音 绕 梁

yú　　yīn　　rào　　liáng

（余，remaining；音，sound；绕，go around；梁，beam）

THE MUSIC LINGERS IN THE AIR LONG
AFTER THE PERFORMANCE

春秋时候，有一位著名的女歌手叫韩娥，有一年，她从韩国到齐国去，一路上把所带的路费全用光了，连吃饭钱都没有了。她只好卖唱解决食宿问题。

　　有一天，韩娥来到了齐国的雍门，这是个人多，很热闹的地方，她就在这里卖唱。她的歌声清脆嘹亮，婉转动听，吸引了好多好多人，博得了阵阵的掌声。演唱结束了，韩娥走了，但是还有许多人仍然聚集在这里，不肯离去。人们都觉得她的歌声仿佛一直在这里的房梁间缭绕着。三天过去了，她的歌声还是飘荡不息。

　　一天，她要住旅店。旅店老板瞧不起她，还欺负她，很蛮横地说：

　　"你这个臭卖唱的，我这里没有你住的地方！"

　　"我怎么不能在这里住呢？"韩娥很气愤地反问。

　　韩娥感到很委屈，伤心地边哭边唱。她的歌声充满着真实的感情，惊动了周围的很多人，听起来很是感动人。不少男女老少都掉下了眼泪；也有的人一连三天都吃不下饭。

　　后来，大家把韩娥请回来，招待她吃饭、住宿。韩娥很受感动，便用歌声报答大家。她那优美欢乐的歌声，使很多人忘记了早先的忧愁，这时都高兴得情不自禁地跳起舞、唱起歌来。于是，大家给韩娥凑足了路费，送她上路，但是韩娥动听的歌声久久留在那里。

　　后来人们根据这个故事引申出"余音绕梁"这句成语，形容人的歌声非常优美，给人留下久久不能忘记的印象。

During the Spring and Autumn Period, there was a famous female singer named Han'e. One year, when she travelled from the State of Han to the State of Qi, she spent all of her money and was forced to sing for money to get food and a place to stay.

One day, Han'e came to sing at the Gate of Harmony, a lively place with throngs of people. Clear and sweet, her voice attracted many listeners, who heartily applauded her. Han'e finished singing and left, but many people remained gathered there, not wanting to depart. It seemed to everyone that her voice was lingering in the beams of the great gate. Even after three days, her singing was still wafting through the air.

One day Han'e needed to stay at an inn. The innkeeper looked at her with scorn and derided her, saying, "You stinking singing wench, there's no place for you here!"

"Why am I not able to stay here?" Han'e asked indignantly.

Feeling very wronged, Han'e began to sing, interspersed with tears. Her voice, full of authentic emotion, startled those around her, who were terribly moved as they listened. Men and women, old and young shed tears, and some couldn't eat for three days afterwards.

Later, everyone invited Han'e to come back, treating her to meals and a place to sleep. Han'e was moved by their kindness, which she repaid with song. That beautiful and merry voice made people forget their worries, and many were so happy that they danced or sang. Later, everyone chipped in and gave Han'e enough money to continue her journey. They saw her on her way, but the beautiful sound of her voice remained for a long, long time.

The idiom "the music lingers in the air long after the performance" is used to describe someone's singing as being exceptionally beautiful and making an unforgettable impression on people.

鹬 蚌 相 争　渔 翁 得 利

yù bàng xiāng zhēng　yú wēng dé lì

(鹬, snipe; 蚌, clam; 相, each other; 争, grapple;
渔翁, fisherman; 得, gain; 利, profits)

WHEN THE SNIPE AND THE CLAM GRAPPLE, ITS THE FISHERMAN WHO STANDS TO BENEFIT

太阳照在大地上，一只大河蚌慢慢地爬上了河滩，张开自己的两扇椭圆形的甲壳晒太阳。它感到非常舒服，悠闲自在。

在离这里不远的水草丛中，有一只大鹬鸟，正迈着两条又长又细的腿，伸着又长又尖的嘴巴，在细心地寻找鱼虫。忽然，它看见河滩上那只张着口的大河蚌。河蚌那鲜嫩、肥美的肉吸引着它，这是多么好吃的美食啊。

鹬鸟悄悄地走过去，伸出它的大嘴巴，猛地啄住了甲壳内的蚌肉。河蚌突然受到了袭击，急忙将坚硬的甲壳闭合，甲壳象把钳子似的紧紧夹住鹬的长嘴巴。鹬鸟用尽全身力气想拉出蚌肉来。河蚌却死死地夹住鹬嘴。就这样，鹬蚌之间展开了一场激烈的搏斗。

鹬鸟和河蚌谁也不肯让谁，相持不下，双方争吵起来。鹬鸟威胁河蚌说：

"你若不张开甲壳，今天不下雨，明天也不下雨，你会被晒死在这里的，赶快张开甲壳吧！"

河蚌也不示弱地说："我就是不张开甲壳，我把你狠狠地夹住，你今天拔不出来，明天也拔不出来，你就非憋死在这河滩上。"

鹬鸟和河蚌互不相让，死死地纠缠在一起。

正在这时，一个老渔夫从河滩路过，看见鹬蚌相争，没有费多大力气，把它们两个一起抓住，高兴地拿回家了。

后来人们根据这个故事引申出"鹬蚌相争，渔翁得利"这句成语，用来比喻双方不和、互相争斗，结果两败俱伤，让第三者占了便宜。

As the sun beats down on the earth, a freshwater clam slowly climbs up on the bank of a river. Opening the two halves of its fan-shaped shell, it basked in the sunlight, comfortable and care-free.

In the reeds not far from there was a large snipe who was walking along on its long, spindly legs, using its long, pointed beak to search meticulously for water fleas. Suddenly, it spied the clam lying there with its shell open on the bank of the river. The tender and sweet meat of the clam drew it's attention — what a nice treat!

The snipe stole over and, sticking out its great beak, quickly took hold of the clam's flesh. The clam, upon receiving such a surprise attack, quickly slammed its hard shell closed, trapping the snipe's beak as tight as a pair of pliers. The snipe used nearly all its strength to try to pull the meat out, but the clam was locked fast around the snipe's beak. Thus an intense battle unfolded between the snipe and the clam.

The snipe and the clam were locked in a stalemate, with neither willing to give in to the other. The two started to argue.

"It won't rain today and it won't rain tomorrow. If you don't open your shell, you'll be roasted to death in this sun. Open your shell!" the snipe threatened.

The clam didn't back down. "I'm not opening my shell. I'm holding you tight. You can't pull me out today, you can't pull me out tomorrow, and you will starve to death on this river bank!" it said.

Neither snipe nor clam would yield, and they remained entangled together.

Just then, an old fisherman happened to be walking along the river bank. With not much effort, he trapped both snipe and clam and happily took them home.

The idiom "when the snipe and the clam grapple, it's the fisherman who stands to benefit" is a metaphor for a third party gaining from two parties fighting a victorless struggle.

争 先 恐 后

zhēng　xiān　kǒng　hòu

(争, strive; 先, first; 恐, fear; 后, lag behind)

STRIVE TO BE THE FIRST
AND FEAR TO LAG BEHIND

春秋时期，晋国有一个赶车能手名叫王良，他的赶车技术很高超，由他赶的车既轻快又稳当，人们都愿意坐他的车。

王良会赶车的事，后来被晋国的贵族赵襄子知道了，就请他到家里，向他学赶车的本领。赵襄子学了几天，就以为学得不错了，便提出来要与王良比赛，王良只好答应。

比赛时，赵襄子选了最好的马、最好的车参加比赛。赵襄子坐在华丽的车上，驾驶高头大马，显得非常威风。而王良的马、车显得很逊色。

比赛开始了，两个人分头赶着车飞快地跑着。赵襄子使劲地甩鞭子打马，开始跑得很快，但时间不长就落在王良的车后了。第一次比赛赵襄子输了，他以为是马没有选好，不如王良的马。于是，他换了一匹马又比赛，又输了。再提出第三次比赛，这次赵襄子既换马又换车，结果他又输了。赵襄子败兴极了。

赵襄子以质问的口气说：

"你教我赶车，为什么不把本领全都教给我呢？"

王良很坦然地说：

"我赶车的本领，是毫无保留地全都教给你了。我曾经跟你说过，赶车最重要的是让马与车协调，马套在车辕上要合适，使马感到舒服，马在跑时还要不断调整，使马和车配合好。赶车时要沉住气，要把心思都集中在马身上，使人和马调理一致，能做到赶起车来得心应手。这样才能跑得快、跑得远。可是你不是这样，你的心思不是在马、车上。当你赶车跑在前面时，心里想的只是怕我赶上你；当你落在我的后边时，心里又想怕赶不上我，这样争先恐后地把注意力都集中在我身上了，这样，你哪还有心思把马和车协调配合好呢，这就是你赶车落后的原因。"

赵襄子听了感到很有道理。

后来人们根据这个故事引申出"争先恐后"这句成语，比喻人们遇事争着向前，唯恐落后。

During the Spring and Autumn Period, there was a crack chariot driver from the State of Jin named Wang Liang. Due to his superior skill, when he drove chariots, the ride was always smooth and steady. Everyone wanted to ride with him.

A Jin aristocrat named Zhao Xiangzi heard of Wang Liang's talents and invited him to his house to learn driving skills from him. After a few days of learning, Zhao Xiangzi thought he was already pretty good, and proposed a race between him and Wang Liang. Wang Liang could only agree.

For the competition, Zhao Xiangzi chose the best horse and the best chariot. Sitting on his resplendent chariot drawn by a grand, high-headed horse, he looked magnificent. Wang Liang's horse and chariot looked shabby in comparison.

The race started, and both men sped off in their chariots. Zhao Xiangzi whipped his horse forcefully, and it ran quickly at first. But after a moment it began to fall behind Wang Liang. Zhao Xiangzi lost the first race. He thought it was because he hadn't chosen a good horse, that his horse wasn't as good as Wang Liang's. So they switched horses and raced again, and Zhao Xiangzi lost again. In a third race, they switched both horses and chariots, but the result was the same, and Zhao Xiangzi was terribly disappointed.

He tried to call Wang Liang to account, asking, "You taught me how to drive a chariot, but why didn't you teach me everything?"

Wang Liang answered frankly:

"I taught you everything I know. I told you before, the most important thing in driving a chariot is to coordinate the horse and the chariot. The horse's harness must be well suited to the chariot's shaft so that the horse will feel comfortable. When the horse is running, continual adjustments must be made to synchronize horse and chariot. While driving, you must remain calm and concentrate your heart and mind on the horse, making both rider and horse feel at ease. Only in this way will the horse be able to run fast and far. But you did not do this. Your thoughts and feelings were not on the horse and chariot. When you pulled out in front, you were only afraid that I would catch up. When you fell behind, you were only afraid that you wouldn't catch up with me. This striving to be the first and fearing to lag behind made you put all your attention on me, and you couldn't concentrate on synchronizing the horse and chariot. This is why you always came in last."

Zhao Xiangzi felt this made sense.

Now the idiom "strive to be the first and fear to lag behind" is used to describe those who take such an attitude when dealing with situations.

郑 人 买 履

zhng   rén   mǎi   lǔ

（郑，name of a kingdom; 人，man; 买，buy; 履，shoes）

THE MAN FROM ZHENG BUYS SHOES

古时候，郑国有个人，他的鞋破了，想买双新鞋。他在家里，先用尺比着自己的脚量个尺码，再找了根稻草，量成同样长的尺码，然后带着尺码去买鞋。

这一天，正是赶集的日子，这个人急于赶路，匆匆忙忙地来到集市上。他找到卖鞋的地方，看到有合适的鞋，很满意。正想要买鞋，他摸摸口袋，又上下摸摸全身，自言自语地说：

"哎呀！不好！我忘记带尺码了。那根记尺码的稻草准是忘在家中的凳子上了。"

他马上又对卖鞋的人说：

"我没有带鞋的尺码，等我回家把尺码拿来再买。"

说完，他拔脚急忙往家跑。

卖鞋的人见他跑远了，心想：他准是替别人代买鞋。

他回家拿了尺码，又慌慌张张地跑到集市，这样一来一去花了不少时间，等他气喘吁吁地赶到集市时，天已晚了，集市已经散了，卖鞋的人也走了。他白白地跑了两趟，还是没有买到鞋。

这件事被邻居知道了，就问他：

"你是给自己买鞋呢？还是替别人代买鞋呢？"

他自信地回答：

"是给自己买的。"

邻居听了感到很奇怪，就说：

"你没有带尺码，可有脚呀，你为什么不用自己的脚去试试鞋的大小呢？"

他又说：

"我相信自己量过的尺码是很准确的，至于我自己的脚吗？那就不一定可靠了。"

邻居都笑了，有人说：

"怎么连自己的脚也不相信了，真是笑话。"

后来人们根据这个笑话引申出"郑人买履"这句成语，讽喻那些只相信教条，不顾客观实际的人。

In ancient times there was a man from the State of Zheng. His shoes were worn out and he wanted to buy a new pair. At home, he used a ruler to measure the size of his feet. Then he took a rice stalk and measured out the same length. Then he took the rice stalk showing his foot size to go buy some shoes.

That day happened to be a market day, and the man hurried along the road, hastening to the market. He found the shoe section and saw a suitable pair of shoes that he liked. Just as he was going to buy them he felt in his pocket, then searched his whole person, saying aloud to himself, "Aiya! I forgot to bring my size along! That stalk of rice measuring my foot size is on the stool at home!"

He quickly said to the shoe seller, "I didn't bring my shoe size along. Wait for me to go home and get it."

With that, he sped off back home.

As the shoe seller watched him race into the distance he thought, "He must be buying shoes for somebody else."

After the man got the measurement, he hurried back to the market. A lot of time had already gone by, and when he arrived panting at the market, the sky was already dark, the market had broken up, and the shoe seller already gone. He had made the trip twice in vain.

When the man's neighbor heard about this, he asked him, "Were you buying shoes for yourself, or for someone else?"

The man replied confidently, "For myself!"

The neighbor felt this to be a little strange and said, "You may not have had your measurements, but you had your feet didn't you? Why didn't you just try on the shoes to see if they fit?"

The man said, "I trust that my measurements are accurate, but as for my own feet? They're not so reliable."

The neighbor laughed and said, "How can you not believe in your own feet? What a ridiculous thing!"

Later, this joke gave rise to the idiom, "the man from Zheng buys shoes", which satirizes those who only believe in dogma and don't consider objective reality.

纸 上 谈 兵

zhǐ　shàng　tán　bīng

（纸，paper; 上，on; 谈，discuss; 兵，art of war）

FIGHT ONLY ON PAPER

战国时期，赵国有一员大将名叫赵奢，曾打败过秦国的军队，为赵国立过大功。

赵奢有个儿子名叫赵括，从小受父亲的影响，跟父亲学习兵法，很多兵书都能背诵下来，当同别人谈起用兵打仗的事时，说的滔滔不绝，条条是理，谁也比不上他，就连他的父亲也说不过他。日子久了，赵括就以为天下没有人能比得上他了。

由于很多人夸奖赵括，他的母亲也非常高兴，可是，赵奢从来不夸奖他。有一次赵括的母亲问道：

"咱们的儿子到底怎么样？"

赵奢说："打仗本来是最复杂，最危险的事，哪有象他说的那么轻松、容易。他是纸上谈兵，没有多大本领，如果以后他真的当上大将军，领兵作战，赵国的军队就要毁在他的手里。"

后来，秦国攻打赵国，这时赵奢已经死去，赵王派老将廉颇率兵抵抗。廉颇率兵打退秦军后，就修筑工事，坚守阵地，采取防守的办法，想把秦国军队拖垮，再打败他们。

秦军一时难以攻破赵国，就想出一条计策，派人到赵国，散布流言，说廉颇胆小，不难对付，秦军最怕赵括。赵王中计了，听信了谣言，便派赵括代替廉颇作大将军，来统率全军。赵括的母亲知道后，赶忙来劝赵王，说：

"赵奢生前说过，赵括虽然读过兵书，但没有带兵打仗的实际经验，只会夸夸其谈，纸上谈兵，可千万不能派他去。"可是，赵王坚持不听。

赵括到前线后，更加趾高气扬，无故改变了廉颇的战略，撤换了将领，一切按兵书上说的办。秦军了解到这些情况后，立即派出一支军队，假装败退，实际上是把赵军运粮草的道路断绝。在秦军的引诱下，赵括以为秦军真的败退了，马上率领全军出击。结果，赵军被秦军团团围住40多天，粮食吃完了，马料也没了，上下军心大乱。平日熟读兵法的赵括也无办法了，只好带兵拼命突围。赵括被乱箭射死了，赵军没有了主帅，最后全军覆没。赵国大伤元气，从此就衰弱下去了。

后来人们根据这个故事引申出"纸上谈兵"这句成语，比喻只会夸夸其谈，空发议论，不能解决实际问题的人；或比喻只是空谈，不能成为现实的事物。

During the Warring States Period, the State of Zhao had a general named Zhao She who once defeated the Qin armies, thus rendering a great service to Zhao.

Zhao She had a son named Zhao Kuo, who grew up under his father's influence, studying the art of war and memorizing a great number of military tracts. Whenever discussing troops and battles he could let forth a stream of eloquence and reason such that none could compare with him, and even his father couldn't best him in arguement. As time went on, Zhao Kuo began to think that no one could match him.

Because so many people commended Zhao Kuo, his mother was very happy. But Zhao She never praised his son. Once Zhao Kuo's mother asked him, "What do you really think of our son?"

Zhao She answered, "War is the most complex, dangerous thing in the world. It is not nearly so light and easy as he makes it sound. He can fight on paper, which doesn't take much skill. If he were really to be a general and direct real soldiers in a real battle, the Zhao armies would be destroyed in his hands."

Some time later, when Zhao She had already passed away, the State of Qin attacked Zhao. The king dispatched the seasoned general Lian Po to resist. After repulsing the Qin troops, Lian Po had defensive fortifications built to hold the position of the Zhao troops. By using defensive tactics, Lian Po hoped to wear down the Qin armies and then defeat them.

The Qin were temporarily at a loss as to how to breakthrough Zhao's defenses. Then they came up with a plan: send someone to Zhao to spread the word that Lian Po was a coward and no match for the Qin, but that the Qin were really afraid of Zhao Kuo. The king of Zhao fell for the trick, believing the rumors. He sent Zhao Kuo to take over from Lian Po as general in command of all the armies. When Zhao Kuo's mother heard the news, she hurried to the king.

"When Zhao She was alive he said that while Zhao Kuo has read military books, he has never had any practical experience leading troops in battle. Zhao She said that he can only indulge in verbiage and fight on paper, and never, ever send him into an actual war," she said.

But the king didn't listen.

When Zhao Kuo arrived at the front lines, he strutted around swollen with arrogance, altering Lian Po's strategies without proper reason. He recalled all the commanders and arranged everything as it was written in the military texts. When the Qin heard about this, they immediately sent out a battalion, which pretended to be defeated. In fact, they cut off Zhao Kuo's supply lines. Lured into thinking the Qin army was really in retreat, Zhao Kuo immediately led his whole army in an attack. As a result, the Zhao army found themselves completely surrounded, remaining so for over 40 days. Their rations and horse feed were out of supply and troop morale plummeted. Zhao Kuo, who had spent his days learning military books, was at a loss. All he could do was leading his soldiers in one last-ditch attempt to break the seige. Zhao Kuo died, shot full of arrows. Left without a commander, the Zhao army was annihilated. The vitality of the State of Zhao was dealt a major blow and it began a descent into weakness.

The idiom "fight only on paper" is used to describe someone who is given over to verbiage or empty discussion and is unable to deal with practical problems. It is also used as a metaphor for empty talk that is unable to become something real.

指 鹿 为 马

zhǐ　lù　wéi　mǎ

（指，point to；鹿，stag；为，as；马，horse）

CALL A STAG A HORSE

秦始皇死后，他的小儿子胡亥继承了王位，称为秦二世。秦始皇的大臣赵高做了丞相。赵高是有名的奸臣。当时，他已经窃取了秦王朝的实权，但还不甘心，野心很大，想趁秦二世刚当了皇帝，地位还不稳的时候，废了他，自己当皇帝。可是他想：若是朝廷的大臣不服气，反对我怎么办呢？于是，他想出了一个办法来试探一下，看看到底有多少大臣顺从他，多少大臣反对他。

有一天，赵高趁文武百官早晨朝见秦二世的时候，让他手下人牵了一头鹿，献给秦二世，赵高故意说：

"这是一匹千里马，特意敬送给陛下的。"

秦二世先是一愣，随后大笑了，说：

"丞相，你搞错了，怎么把梅花鹿说成是千里马呢？"

赵高一本正经地说：

"陛下，这的确是一匹马。"

"马怎么会长角呢？"秦二世反驳他说。

赵高还是坚持说：

"这就是马，不然，请诸位大臣辨认一下，你们都说说这是鹿呢，还是马？"

这本来是一目了然的事，但是，文武百官中每个人的态度却不一样。有些一直追随赵高和想讨好赵高的大臣便跟着说："这肯定是一匹好马。"有些怕得罪赵高的大臣不敢说实话，但也不能违背自己的良心，只好不作声。有些正直的大臣，已经看出赵高的险恶用心，就尊重事实，说："是鹿。"

赵高通过这次试探，摸到了底，他看出，凡是说实话的，不同意他"指鹿为马"的大臣，都是反对他的人。事后，赵高便强加种种罪名，一一加以暗害，从此大臣们更加害怕赵高了。不久，赵高派人谋杀了秦二世。

后来人们根据这个事件引申出"指鹿为马"这句成语。比喻怀着恶意，有意颠倒黑白，混淆是非。

After the death of Qin Shihuang, his son Hu Hai ascended to the throne and took the imperial name of Qin Ershi (the second emperor of Qin). A high advisor of Qin Shihuang's, Zhao Gao, became prime minister. Zhao Gao is infamous for his treachery. He had already usurped the real authority of the Qin court, but he wasn't content. With great ambition, he thought to take advantage of Qin Ershi's new and unstable position as emperor to depose him and make himself emperor. But he also thought about the possibility of other ministers in the court opposing him. Therefore, he thought up a way to test how many ministers would go along with him and how many would oppose him.

One day, when the emperor was having a morning court audience with all the civil and military officials, Zhao Gao had a subordinate bring in a stag to present to Qin Ershi. Zhao Gao said, "This is a fine steed that I would like to present to Your Majesty."

Qin Ershi was dumbfounded for a moment. Then he laughed and said, "Prime Minister, you are mistaken. How can you call a stag a horse?"

Zhao Gao replied seriously, "Your Majesty, this is most definitely a horse."

"How can a horse grow horns?" Qin Ershi countered.

Zhao Gao persisted, "This is a horse. If not, let us ask the other ministers to make an identification. Do you say this is a stag? Or a horse?"

This originally was a very clear case, but attitudes among the officials were quite different. Those who were directly aligned with Zhao Gao or wanted to fawn on him said, "This is definitely a horse." There were those who were afraid of Zhao Gao and afraid to speak the truth, but who were unable to ignore their consciences and thus didn't speak out. Some upright ministers saw through Zhao Gao's sinister intentions and honored the truth, saying, "This is a stag."

Zhao Gao could see from this test that all those who spoke the truth, opposing his claim that the stag was a horse, were those who opposed him. After this incident, Zhao Gao raised every kind of false accusation against these men, stabbing them in the back one by one. The ministers became even more afraid of Zhao Gao and not long after, he had someone assassinate Qin Ershi.

The idiom "call a stag a horse" means, with malicious purpose, to intentionally invert black and white and mix up truth and fiction.

趾 高 气 扬

zhǐ gāo qì yáng

(趾, toe; 高, high; 气扬, puff one's chest out)

STRUT ABOUT AND GIVE ONESELF AIRS

春秋时期，楚国有一名将领名叫屈瑕，人很勇敢，也能指挥打仗。有一年，楚国派他率领军队攻打绞国，最后打了一个大胜仗。从此，屈瑕就骄傲起来了，自以为很了不起。

第二年，楚王又派屈瑕率领军队去攻打罗国。出征那天，文武官员为他送行，祝贺他再打胜仗。屈瑕在一片赞扬声中，摆出不可一世的样子，显得更神气十足，连走路都把脚抬得高高的。

大臣斗伯比也去给屈瑕送行了。在坐车回来时，他对车夫说："你看屈瑕目空一切的样子，一个带兵打仗的人怎么能这么高傲，并没有把敌人放在心上。他不是以意志坚定的心理去打仗，这次一定会打败仗的。"

斗伯比回来后，马上去见楚王，他说：

"请大王赶快派援军，去帮助屈瑕吧。"

楚王感到很奇怪，就说：

"屈瑕刚出征，哪能派援军呢，胡闹！"

楚王并没有接受斗伯比的建议。

楚王回到宫中后，同他的夫人提起此事，说斗伯比有些古怪，他的建议是什么意思呢？楚王夫人分析说：

"我看斗伯比的用意并不在于派援军，而是他已经看出屈瑕高傲、自负、轻敌，这次一定打败仗。你应该马上派些人去告诫屈瑕。"

楚王立刻派人追回屈瑕，但是已经来不及了。事情正如斗伯比预见到的，由于屈瑕盲目自信，骄傲轻敌，又麻痹大意，当楚军进入罗国时毫无警惕，就遭到罗国军队的两面夹攻，紧紧包围，最后惨败。这时，楚王派的人还没有赶到。

后来人们根据这个故事引申出"趾高气扬"这句成语，来比喻得意忘形，骄傲自大的样子。

During the Spring and Autumn Period, there was a general from the State of Chu named Qu Xia who was very brave and capable in directing battles. One year he was sent to attack the State of Jiao, and won a great victory. From then on, Qu Xia grew arrogant, and thought himself quite extraordinary.

The next year, the king of Chu again sent Qu Xia to lead an attack, this time against the State of Luo. On the day the army was to set out, all the court officials came to see Qu Xia off and wish him victory. Amidst all the praise and admiration, Qu Xia put on airs of insufferable arrogance. As he walked, he stepped high, appearing proud and triumphant.

A minister named Dou Bobi was among those seeing Qu Xia off. Returning in a chariot, he said to the driver, "Look at how Qu Xia acts as though everyone is beneath him. How can one who leads troops display such arrogance? He has not considered the enemy in his heart. He is not going to battle with a resolute will. This time he will lose."

When Dou Bobi returned, he immediately went to see the king.

"Your Majesty should quickly send reinforcements to help Qu Xia," Dou Bobi said.

The king thought this quite peculiar, and said, "Nonsense! Qu Xia has only just set out. Why should we send reinforcements?"

The king did not accept Dou Bobi's suggestion.

When the king returned to his palace, he brought the matter up with his wife, saying he thought Dou Bobi was a little strange. What did he mean by his suggestion? The king's wife gave an analysis:

"It seems to me that Dou Bobi's purpose lies not in sending troops but rather that he perceived that Qu Xia's arrogance, conceit, and underestimation of the enemy would lead to defeat in this battle. You should send someone right away to warn Qu Xia."

The king immediately dispatched someone to recall Qu Xia, but it was too late. The situation turned out exactly as Dou Bobi predicted. Because of Qu Xia's blind confidence and arrogant disregard of the enemy, he was caught off his guard. As the Chu troops moved into Luo they were careless and fell into a pincer attack by the Luo army. Tightly encircled, they suffered a terrible defeat. By that time, the king's messenger hadn't even arrived.

The idiom "strut about and give oneself airs" was drawn from this story to mean one who has been swollen by past successes.

朝 三 暮 四

zhāo　　sān　　mù　　sì

（朝, morning; 三, three; 暮, evening; 四, four)

BLOW HOT AND COLD

从前，有一位老人非常喜爱猴子，便在家里饲养了一群猴子。他天天与猴子生活在一起，时间长了，就从猴子的一举一动中，掌握了它的习性。那些猴子也慢慢地懂得了主人的意思。老人教猴子杂耍动作，猴子一学就会，还常给老人表演。从而老人更加喜爱这群猴子。宁肯节省家里的口粮，每天自己少吃，也要把猴子喂养好，从不让猴子饿着。

后来，老人家里的口粮越来越少了，只好给猴子吃橡子。再以后，橡子也在减少，但又怕猴子不答应、不听话，怎么办呢？有一天早上，他便同猴子商量说：

"今后每天给你们吃的橡子，早上吃三颗，晚上吃四颗，够吃吗？"

猴子一听，又吵又闹，嚷着：

"不够，不够，这太少了。"

老人灵机一动，转念一想，便改口对猴子说：

"早上三颗，晚上四颗你们嫌少，那么就再增加一颗，让大家都吃饱。"从今以后，每天早晨吃四颗，晚上吃三颗，这样你们都该满意了吧。"

猴子一听，原来早上只发给三颗，现在增加到四颗，果然是增加了一颗，都十分满意，高兴得又蹦又跳，跑到主人跟前领取橡子吃了。

后来人们根据这个故事引申出"朝三暮四"这句成语。无论是朝三暮四也好，还是朝四暮三也好，但总的数目是没有变化。原表现一种欺骗的手法；后来比喻经常变化，反反复复，使人捉摸不定。

Once upon a time there was an old man who loved monkeys and raised a good number of them in his home. After having lived with monkeys every day for a long time, he grew to understand their habits and tendencies. The monkeys also slowly came to understand their master. The old man taught his monkeys some tricks and acts. The monkeys rapidly mastered them, often performing for the old man, who grew to love the monkeys even more. He preferred to cut down on his own grain rations in order to feed the monkeys better. Every day he ate little, but never let the monkeys go hungry.

As time went on, the old man's grain rations were reduced more and more until he had to start giving the monkeys acorns. Soon the acorns were becoming depleted, too, but he was afraid the monkeys wouldn't take it well. What could he do? One morning he talked it over with the monkeys.

"From today on I'll give you three acorns in the morning and four in the evening. Will that be enough?" the old man asked.

The monkeys made a big fuss and grumbled, "Not enough, not enough! That's too little!"

The old man thought for a second and had a flash of inspiration.

He said, "If three in the morning and four in the evening is not enough for you, then I'll add one and let everyone eat his fill. From now on, every morning you'll get *four* acorns, and in the evening you'll get three. Does this satisfy everyone?"

The monkeys thought about it: originally they would only get three acorns in the morning; now they would get four, or one more. They were very satisfied and so happy they bounced and jumped around, running to their master's feet to get their acorns.

The idiom "blow hot and cold" originally signify some kind of deception, but later came to mean always changing, making it difficult for people to ascertain one's meaning.

自 相 矛 盾

zì xiāng máo dùn

（自，oneself；相，each other；矛盾，contradict）

CONTRADICT ONESELF

在中国古代，作战打仗使用的武器中有矛有盾。矛是用来刺杀敌人，进攻用的长枪；而盾是用来遮挡身子，防御敌人的矛刺中的挡牌。

　　当时，楚国有个卖矛又卖盾的人。有一天，他背着矛和盾在街上叫卖，为了让大家买自己的货，他先举起盾来，向人夸耀说：

　　"我这种盾呀，是非常坚固的，无论怎么锋利的矛也不能把它刺破的。"

　　说了几遍后，他见围观的人没有什么反应，便又举起他的矛向众人夸口说：

　　"再请大家瞧一瞧我的这杆矛，再锋利不过了，不管是多么坚固的盾都挡不住，都会被它刺穿的。"

　　围观的人们听他这样地自吹自夸，都哈哈地笑了。这时，有个人问他：

　　"照你这样说：你的矛是最锋利的，不管多么硬的盾都能刺穿，你的盾是最坚固的，无论怎样锋利的矛也不能被刺破，如果用你的矛戳你的盾，结果会怎么样呢！"

　　这么一问，这个卖矛和盾的人张口结舌，哑口无言，回答不上来了，只好收拾起矛和盾，红着脸走开了。

　　根据这个故事，后来人们就把彼此互相抵触、互相对立的情况叫做矛盾。自己说话、办事前后不一致，相互违背都可说是"自相矛盾"，并引申出了"自相矛盾"这句成语。

Some of the weapons of war in ancient China included the *mao* and the *dun*. The *mao* was a kind of long spear used for stabbing and attacking, while the *dun* was a kind of shield used for protecting the body and turning spears.

In the ancient State of Chu there was a man who wanted to sell his *mao* (spear) and his *dun* (shield). One day, he carried them out on the street to attract possible buyers. First he held up the shield, boasting, "This shield is so solid that no spear is sharp enough to penetrate it."

After speaking a few more words, he saw that there was no reaction among the crowd. So he lifted up the spear and said to those watching, "Everyone set your eyes on this spear! No spear is sharper than this one! It can pierce any shield, no matter how solid!"

The crowd listened to the man and laughed at his bragging and boasting. Then someone asked, "According to what you say, your spear is so sharp that no matter how hard the shield, it will still pierce it; and your shield is so solid that no matter how sharp the spear, it can't be pierced. Then if you used your spear to jab your shield, what would happen?!?"

At this the seller became tongue-tied and he fumbled for words, but was unable to answer. He could only collect his spear and shield and slink away with a red face.

Today, the word for contradiction in Chinese is *maodun*, and if one's words or actions are at odds with each other, one is said to be *zixiang maodun*, or self-contradictory.

坐 井 观 天

zuò　　jǐng　　guān　　tiān

(坐, sit; 井, well; 观, look; 天, sky)

LOOK AT THE SKY
FROM THE BOTTOM OF A WELL

在通往东海海岸的大路旁边，有一口废井，那里住着一只大青蛙。它就生活在这块小小的天地里，至于井外边有多么大，它是全不知道的。

有一天，青蛙在井边碰见一只从东海来的大海龟，它俩便聊起来了。青蛙自鸣得意地夸口说：

"你看，我在这里是多么快乐呵，当我高兴的时候，就在井台边上跳来跳去；当我跳累了就在井壁砖洞中安安静静地休息或者把身子泡在水中舒舒服服地洗个澡；也可以将身子安安逸逸地飘浮在水中，只把头和嘴露出水面上来；要不就在软绵绵的烂泥里悠闲自在地散散步，也是满舒适的。"

青蛙又指指井里的小蝌蚪和小虫们傲慢地说：

"我是这井里的真正主人，它们都比不上我。我是最幸福、最快乐的。这里是世界上最美好、最快乐、最舒适的地方。"

最后，青蛙邀请海龟到井里来参观：

"热烈欢迎你下井玩玩，观赏观赏我这个美好的乐园。"

海龟听了青蛙的介绍，很想下去参观，可是，刚一迈左脚，还没有伸进去右脚，却已经被井栏绊住了，只好摇摇头，退回来。

海龟便对青蛙说：

"朋友，你去过东海吗，大海可广阔了，几千里远还看不见边际，天连水、水连天。大海可深了，深到几十丈还没有见底，陆地上闹多大的水灾，海水也不会涨出多少来；陆地上怎样干旱，怎么不下雨，海水也不会减少多少。住在那里，才是真正的快乐呢。"

这只井里的青蛙听得目瞪口呆，好半天也说不出话来，它感到自己太渺小了，见识太短浅了。

后来人们根据这个童话故事引申出"坐井观天"（或"井底之蛙"）这句成语，比喻眼界狭小，见识短浅，没有远见的人。

On a road leading to the shore of the East Sea was an old, out-of-use well. In the well lived a frog. The frog lived in his tiny realm, and knew nothing of the vast world outside.

One day the frog saw a turtle that had come from the East Sea, and the two started to chat. The frog boasted:

"Look! I'm so happy here, I can jump around the rim of this well, and when I'm tired I can rest peacefully in a hole in the side or take a nice bath in the water below; I can stretch my body out and float around nice and easy with just my head and mouth sticking out of the water; I can lazily stroll about in the silky mud — that's nice, too."

The frog then pointed to the tadpoles and little insects in the well and said haughtily:

"I am the true master of this well, none of them can compare with me. I am the most fortunate and happy inhabitant. This is the most beautiful, happy, comfortable place on the face of the earth."

At length the frog invited the turtle down into the well to have a look.

"You are warmly welcomed to come down into the well to play and enjoy this beautiful wonderland!" the frog said.

After hearing the frog's enthusiastic speech, the turtle really wanted to take a look. But when it put its left foot forward, it couldn't get its right foot in for catching on the rim of the well. The turtle could only shake its head and back up.

The turtle said to the frog, "Friend, have you been to the East Sea? The sea is broad and vast. For thousands of miles you can't see its edge. The sky and waters meet on the horizon. The sea is incredibly deep — you can't see the bottom for several hundred feet. When there is a great flood on the land, the sea's waters don't even swell. When there is no rain and a drought is over the land, the sea's waters don't shrink. Living there is a true pleasure."

Listening to these words, the frog in the well was struck dumb. For a long time it didn't speak, feeling insignificant and ignorant.

The idiom "look at the sky from the bottom of a well" (or: the frog at the bottom of the well), means to have a narrow view of the world, to have only superficial knowledge of something, or to be short-sighted.

（京）新登字 136 号

图书在版编目（CIP）数据

轻松学成语：中英对照/雍贺编
－北京：新世界出版社，1998.2
ISBN 7 - 80005 - 341 - 5

I.轻··· II.雍··· III.①对外汉语教学 – 语言读物
②汉语 – 成语 – 汉、英 IV.H195.5

策　　划：姜汉忠
责任编辑：宋　鹤
版面设计：朱桉青

轻 松 学 成 语

雍 贺 编

*

新世界出版社出版

（北京百万庄路 24 号）

邮政编码 100037

北京外文印刷厂印刷

中国国际图书贸易总公司发行

（中国北京车公庄西路 35 号）

北京邮政信箱第 399 号　邮政编码 100044

新华书店北京发行所国内发行

1997 年（汉英）第一版　1998 年北京第二次印刷

850 × 1168 毫米 1/32 开本

ISBN 7 - 80005 - 341 - 5/G・075

02200

9 - CE - 3246P